LONDON, NEW YORK, MUNICH,
MELBOURNE, and DELHI

Senior editor Rob Houston
Editors Helen Abramson, Wendy Horobin,
Steve Setford, Rona Skene
Designers David Ball, Peter Laws,
Clare Marshall, Anis Sayyed, Jemma Westing
Illustrators Adam Benton, Stuart Jackson-Carter,
Anders Kjellberg, Simon Mumford
Creative retouching Steve Willis

Picture research Aditya Katyal, Martin Copeland
Jacket design Jessica Bentall,
Laura Brim, Jemma Westing
Jacket design development manager
Sophia M Tampakopoulos Turner
Producer (pre-production) Rebekah Parsons-King
Production controller Mandy Innes

Managing art editor Philip Letsu
Managing editor Gareth Jones
Publisher Andrew Macintyre
Art director Phil Ormerod
Associate publishing director Liz Wheeler
Publishing director Jonathan Metcalf

First American Edition, 2013
Published in the United States by
DK Publishing
4th floor, 345 Hudson Street, New York, New York 10014

13 14 15 16 17 10 9 8 7 6 5 4 3 2 1
001—195144—10/13

A catalog record for this book
is available from the Library of Congress.

ISBN: 978-1-4654-1422-9

DK books are available at special discounts when
purchased in bulk for sales promotions, premiums,
fund-raising, or educational use. For details,
contact: DK Publishing Special Markets,
345 Hudson Street, New York, New York 10014
or SpecialSales@dk.com.

Printed and bound in China by Hung Hing

Discover more at
www.dk.com

CONTENTS

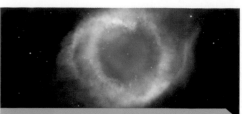

Out of this world

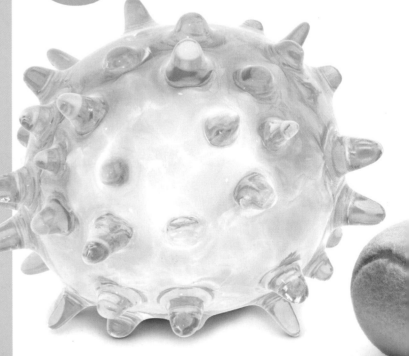

Astounding Earth

Humans and other life-forms

Feats of engineering

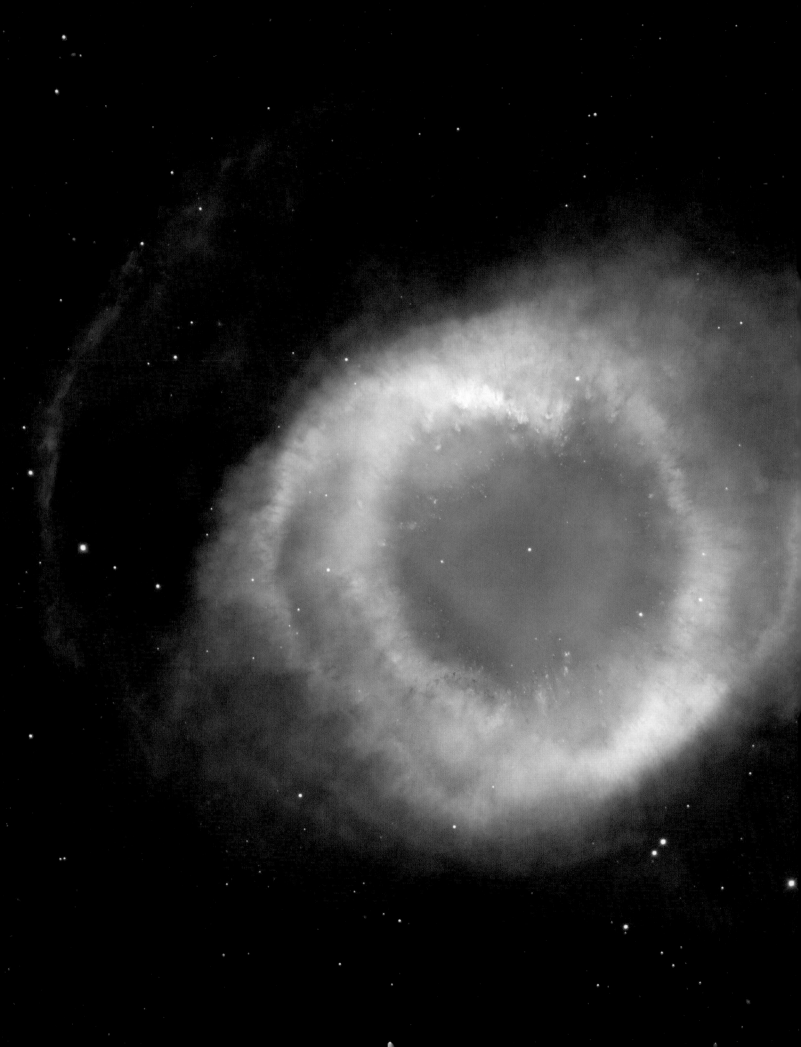

Out of this world

Beyond the safety of planet Earth, space is an incredibly hostile place—vast, airless, and unimaginably cold. But space is also full of amazing things, from fiery stars and weird worlds to mysterious moons, blazing comets, and hurtling asteroids.

The Helix Nebula is made up of huge shells of gas and dust thrown off by a dying star. It is expanding at a rate of nearly 72,000 miles (115,000 kph), which is around 10 times the speed of the fastest-ever aircraft, the rocket-powered North American *X-15*.

How big is the Sun?

The average **diameter** of the **Sun** is **864,337 miles** (1,391,016 km). It is more than **333,000 times** the mass of the **Earth.**

You could fit **109 Earths** across the diameter of the **Sun.**

SUNSPOTS

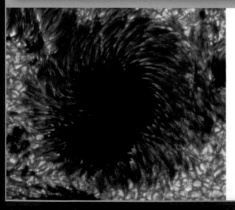

Sunspots are areas where a strong magnetic field stops hot gas reaching the surface. When sunspot numbers increase every 11 years, the Sun's intense magnetic activity can affect radio signals on Earth.

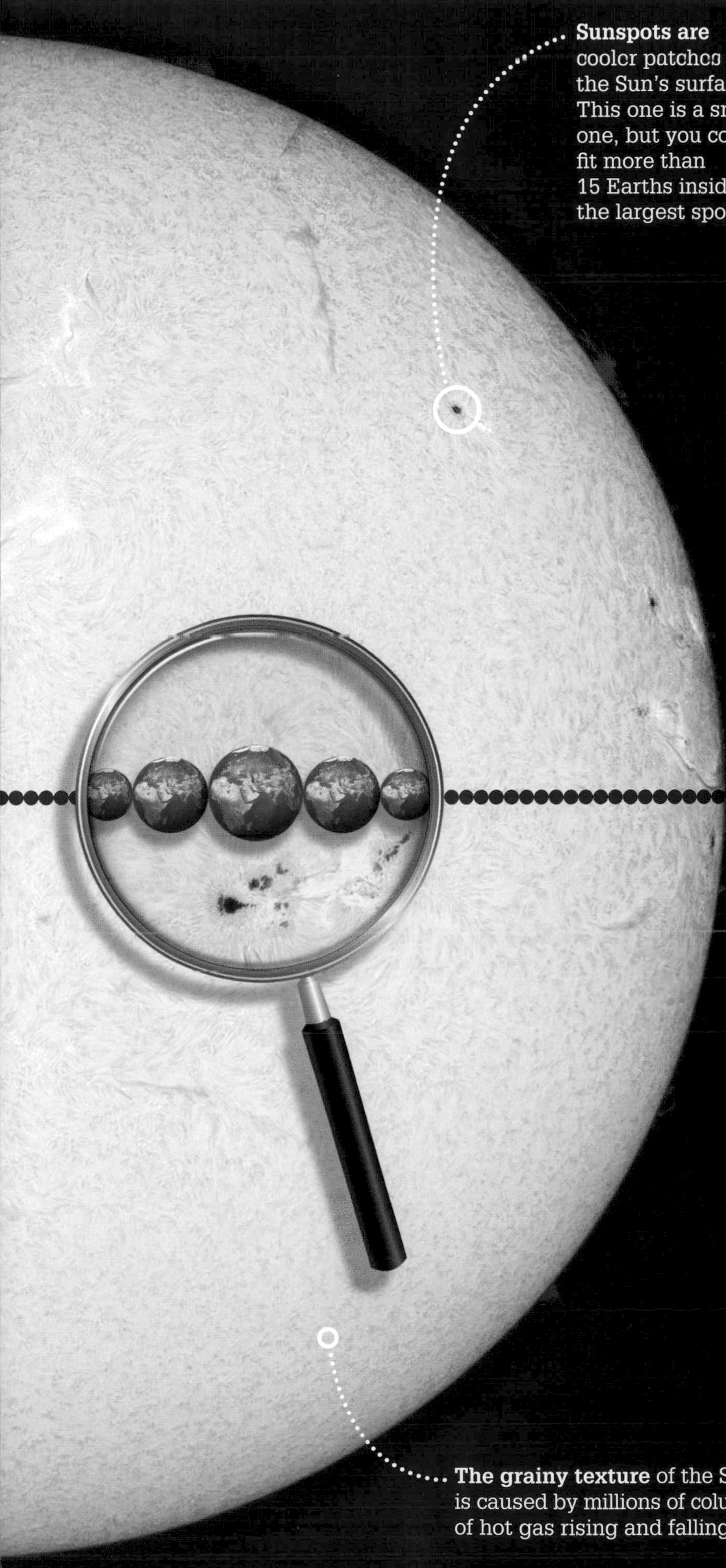

Sunspots are cooler patches on the Sun's surface. This one is a small one, but you could fit more than 15 Earths inside the largest spots.

📈 **FAST FACTS**

Solar flares are eruptions that typically reach 62,000 miles (100,000 km) into space. About eight Earths would fit along one of these flares.

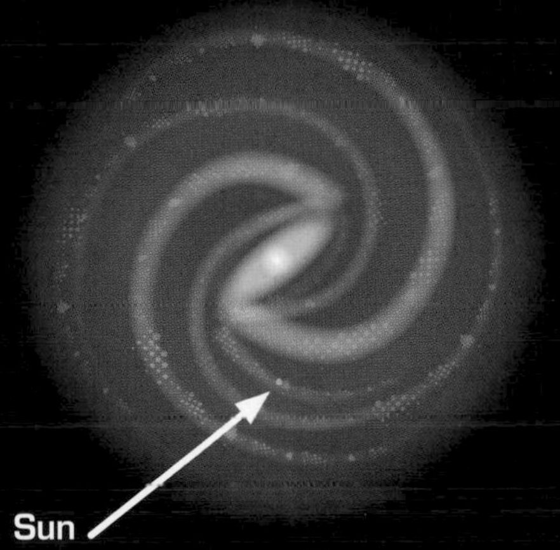

Sun

It takes about 225 million years for the Sun to orbit around the center of the Milky Way. The Sun has made this journey 20 times since it formed around 4.6 billion years ago.

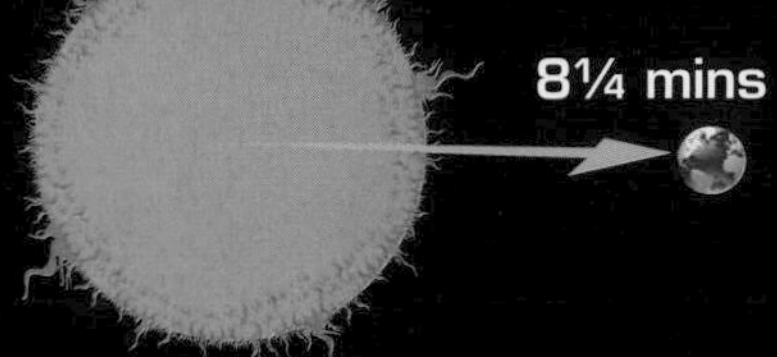

8¼ mins

Light takes about 8¼ minutes to travel from the surface of the Sun to Earth, 43 minutes to get to Jupiter, and around 4¼ hours to reach Neptune.

The grainy texture of the Sun is caused by millions of columns of hot gas rising and falling.

How big is the Moon?

The **Moon's diameter** is **2,159 miles** (3,475 km), **one-quarter** the size of **Earth's**. Its surface area is **13 times smaller.**

The Copernicus Crater, one of the Moon's largest, measures 58 miles (93 km) across.

A PERFECT FIT

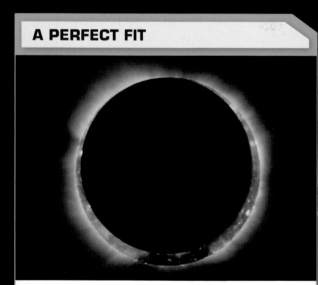

The Sun is 400 times the diameter of the Moon, but, by an amazing coincidence, it is also 400 times farther from the Earth. This means that seen from the Earth during an eclipse, the Sun and the Moon appear to be exactly the same size.

Australia

The Moon is the fifth-largest satellite in the solar system, after three of Jupiter's moons and one of Saturn's. It is the solar system's largest satellite relative to its planet. It doesn't usually hover above Australia, but orbits at a much more distant 238,855 miles (384,400 km) from the Earth.

The Sea of Tranquility is a flat plain of lava that solidified around 4 billion years ago. It is a little larger than the British Isles.

The **Moon is** almost as wide as **Australia,** which is 2,475 miles (3,983 km) across at its widest point.

FAST FACTS

Earth measures 7,926 miles (12,756 km) across at the equator. Four Moons could line up across it.

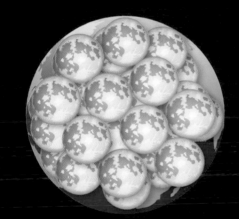

If there were no gaps, 50 Moons could fit inside the globe.

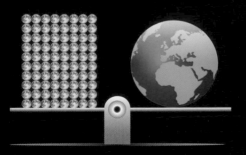

It would take 80 Moons to balance the scales against one Earth. The Earth is so much heavier because its core is solid iron and as wide as two Moons.

How **big** are the planets?

The **planets** in our solar system **vary in size**. Some are **small and rocky**, while others are **enormous balls of gas**.

POISONOUS VENUS

Venus is almost the same size and mass as Earth, but it is very different. Venus has a thick, poisonous atmosphere and a surface temperature of 867°F (464°C), which is hot enough to melt lead.

Jupiter, the biggest planet, measures 86,888 miles (139,833 km) across. It is made mainly of clouds of swirling gas.

The Earth is 7,918 miles (12,742 km) in diameter. It is the largest of the rocky planets and unique for having water on its surface.

📈 FAST FACTS

Venus and Uranus spin in the opposite direction from the other planets. Uranus also rotates on its side, so it appears to spin clockwise or counterclockwise, depending on which pole you're looking at.

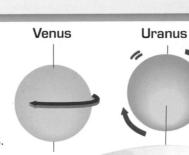

Venus   Uranus

Saturn is the second biggest planet, at 72,367 miles (116,464 km) in diameter. It is made mainly of the gases hydrogen and helium.

Saturn's rings are made up of dust, rock, and ice. They extend 174,000 miles (280,000 km) out, but are just over half a mile (1 km) thick.

Uranus is 31,518 miles (50,724 km) in diameter and is the farthest planet you can see with the naked eye. It is mostly made of gas, but possibly has an icy core.

Neptune is made of very cold gas. The farthest planet from the Sun, it has a diameter of 30,598 miles (49,244 km).

Venus is a rocky planet and, at 7,521 miles (12,104 km) across, is nearly as big as the Earth.

Mercury is 29 times smaller around its equator than Jupiter.

Mars measures 4,225 miles (6,799 km) across. It is known as the "red planet" because of the color of its rusty, iron-rich rocks.

Mercury is the smallest planet, just 3,032 miles (4,879 km) across. It lies the closest to the Sun and is made of rock.

How **big** are the **planets' moons?**

The two **largest moons** in the **solar system** are just over **3,100 miles (5,000 km)** across.

Titan is the only place in the solar system other than Earth to have lakes—although they are made of liquid methane and ethane.

Our **Moon is the fifth largest,** after Jupiter's **Ganymede, Callisto,** and **Io** and Saturn's **Titan.**

Titan
3,200 miles
(5,150 km)

Rhea
950 miles
(1,529 km)

Iapetus
914 miles
(1,471 km)

Dione
698 miles
(1,123 km)

Tethys
662 miles
(1,066 km)

Enceladus
313 miles
(504 km)

Mimas
246 miles (396 km)

SATURN

The Moon
2,159 miles (3,475 km)

EARTH

📈 FAST FACTS

So far, 67 moons have been discovered around Jupiter—the most of any planet. Saturn is second with 62. Uranus has 27 moons, Neptune has 13, Mars has two, and Earth has just one. Venus and Mercury have none.

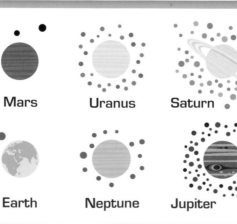

Mars

Uranus

Saturn

Earth

Neptune

Jupiter

HYPERION

Larger moons usually have enough gravity to pull their material into a sphere, or ball shape. Saturn's small moon Hyperion does not have enough gravity, and so its shape is more like a potato.

Ganymede is the largest moon in the solar system—it is bigger than Mercury and three quarters the size of Mars.

Ganymede
3,270 miles
(5,262 km)

Callisto
2,995 miles
(4,821 km)

Triton
1,682 miles
(2,707 km)

Europa
1,940 miles
(3,122 km)

NEPTUNE

Io
2,264 miles
(3,643 km)

JUPITER

Titania
980 miles
(1,578 km)

Oberon
946 miles
(1,523 km)

Both of Mars's tiny moons are possibly ex-asteroids, captured by Mars from the nearby asteroid belt.

Ariel
719 miles
(1,158 km)

Umbriel
726 miles
(1,169 km)

Miranda
293 miles
(472 km)

Deimos
8 miles (12 km)

Phobos
14 miles (22 km)

MARS

URANUS

There are 172 moons orbiting the major planets in the solar system, although new ones are being discovered all the time. Pictured here are each of the planets' major moons. Moons also orbit some dwarf planets, such as Pluto, and even some asteroids.

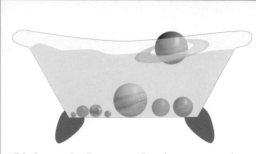

Although Saturn is the second biggest planet, it is not very dense. If you could fill with water a bathtub big enough, Saturn would float. All the other planets, including Jupiter, would sink to the bottom.

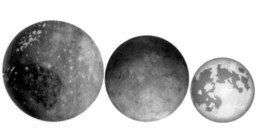

Ganymede   Mercury   Moon

Jupiter has at least 67 moons. The biggest, Ganymede, is also the largest moon in the solar system. It is bigger than the planet Mercury and our own Moon.

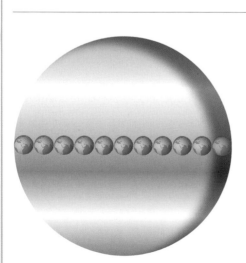

Around 11 Earths would fit across Jupiter's diameter.

Jupiter is made largely of gas, with a small rocky core. It is around two and a half times the combined mass of all the other planets put together.

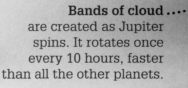

Bands of cloud are created as Jupiter spins. It rotates once every 10 hours, faster than all the other planets.

How **big** is **Jupiter?**

More than **1,320 Earths** would fit inside **Jupiter.**

The **biggest planet** in the solar system is **Jupiter.** It has a **diameter** of **86,888 miles** (139,833 km), a **circumference** of **272,967 miles** (439,298 km) and its total **volume** is **343 trillion cu miles** (1,431 trillion cu km).

GREAT RED SPOT

The Great Red Spot is an enormous storm raging in the atmosphere of Jupiter. It is more than 12,000 miles (20,000 km) wide. You could fit two or three Earths inside it.

How big is an asteroid?

This mountain is one of the tallest peaks in the solar system.

Asteroids range from rocks a few **hundreds of feet** across to the giants **Vesta** (**356 miles**/573 km across) and **Ceres** (**590 miles**/950 km across). **Ceres** is now also classed as a **dwarf planet.**

United States

CHELYABINSK METEOR

If an asteroid enters the Earth's atmosphere, it is called a meteor. In 2013, a meteor about 56 ft (17 m) wide exploded over Russia, shattering windows and damaging buildings with its shock wave.

The chances of something the size of Vesta being on a collision course with Earth are very slim. If it did hit our planet, the impact would be so catastrophic that no life would survive. The asteroid that killed the dinosaurs 65 million years ago was no more than 9 miles (15 km) across.

The surface of Vesta was studied in detail when the *Dawn* spacecraft spent a year orbiting the asteroid in 2011. *Dawn* revealed the surface to be covered in grooves and craters.

... This row of three big craters has been nicknamed the "snowman craters." The snowman's head is facing downward here.

Vesta is as wide as the entire Florida peninsula is long.

Florida

The Bahamas

FAST FACTS

1 Ceres
2 Pallas
3 Juno
4 Vesta
5 Astraea
6 Hebe
7 Iris
8 Flora
9 Metis
10 Hygiea
The Moon

The first 10 asteroids to be discovered were given the numbers 1–10 as part of their name. Even the biggest, Ceres, is much smaller than the Moon.

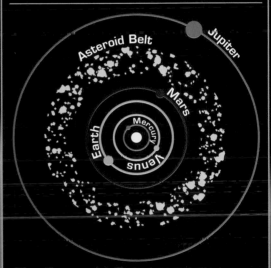

Asteroid Belt   Jupiter
Mars
Mercury
Earth
Venus

The Asteroid Belt between Jupiter and Mars contains millions of different-sized asteroids orbiting the Sun.

Dactyl 4,600 ft (1.4 km) across ↓

Ida 33 miles (54 km) long

Some asteroids have moons. In 1994, for instance, scientists discovered that the asteroid Ida had a small moon, which they named Dactyl.

How big is a comet?

A comet's **nucleus** is **small**, but the **dust** and **gases** that surround it (the **coma**) can be **60,000 miles** (100,000 km) across. Amazingly, the **tail** can be many **millions of miles** long.

CRASH-LANDING

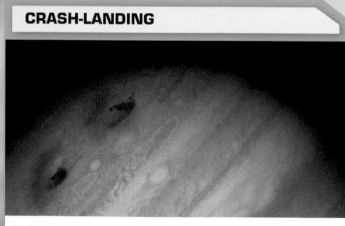

Most comets go around the Sun, but some are captured by Jupiter's massive gravitational pull. In July 1994, comet Shoemaker-Levy 9 broke into pieces and the fragments slammed into Jupiter, leaving a line of dark spots where they hit its atmosphere.

Jupiter
86,888 miles
(139,833 km) across

The tail is made of very thin, glowing gas. There is more matter in 1 cu mm of air than there is in ¼ cu mile (1 cu km) of a comet's tail.

FAST FACTS

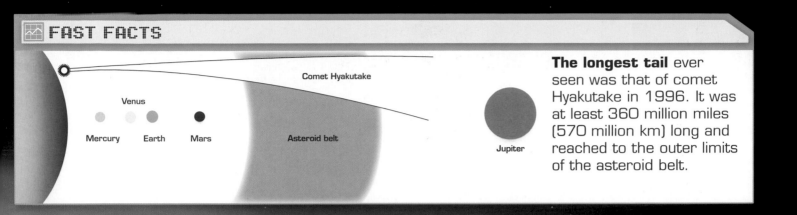

Venus

Mercury   Earth   Mars

Comet Hyakutake

Asteroid belt

Jupiter

The longest tail ever seen was that of comet Hyakutake in 1996. It was at least 360 million miles (570 million km) long and reached to the outer limits of the asteroid belt.

The nucleus of a comet usually measures less than 6 miles (10 km) in diameter. However, it is surrounded by an enormous coma of dust and gases.

A comet's **coma** can spread nearly as wide as **Jupiter**, the **solar system's** largest planet.

Comets spend most of their lives as small, icy bodies orbiting in the outer regions of the solar system. The orbits of some comets, however, send them hurtling inwards. As a comet gets close to the Sun, its ice turns into gas and is blown away from the nucleus by the solar wind, forming a tail.

Where is the biggest canyon?

The Valles Marineris on **Mars** is up to **4 miles** (7 km) **deep** and more than **2,500 miles** (4,000 km) **long**. The **Grand Canyon** would fit along its length **nine times**.

The deepest section of the canyon is the Melas Chasma. It is also the widest area, at about 125 miles (200 km) across.

Valles Marineris is a system of smaller canyons, or "chasmata."

2,500 miles

GRAND CANYON SKYWALK

The Grand Canyon Skywalk is a transparent viewing platfom. Visitors can see through the walkway to the bottom of the canyon 4,000 ft (1,200 m) below.

If the **Valles Marineris were** in North America, it **would stretch** from **Vancouver, Canada, to Boston**.

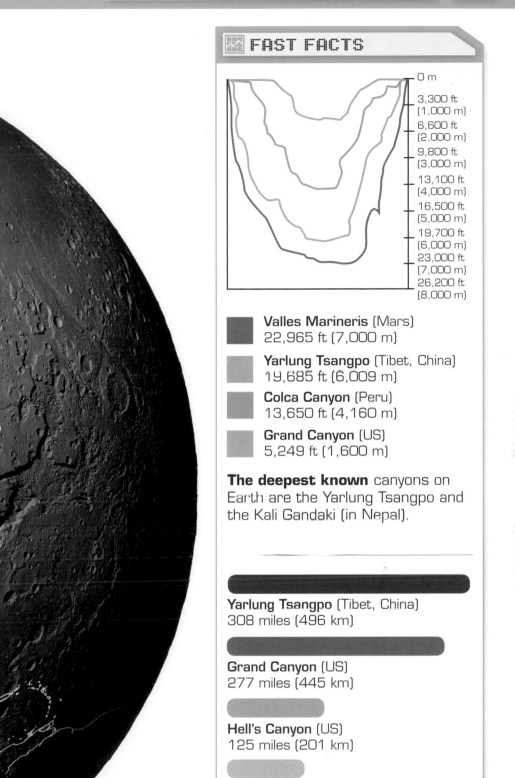

(4,000 km)

FAST FACTS

| 0 m |
| 3,300 ft (1,000 m) |
| 6,600 ft (2,000 m) |
| 9,800 ft (3,000 m) |
| 13,100 ft (4,000 m) |
| 16,500 ft (5,000 m) |
| 19,700 ft (6,000 m) |
| 23,000 ft (7,000 m) |
| 26,200 ft (8,000 m) |

Valles Marineris (Mars)
22,965 ft (7,000 m)

Yarlung Tsangpo (Tibet, China)
19,685 ft (6,009 m)

Colca Canyon (Peru)
13,650 ft (4,160 m)

Grand Canyon (US)
5,249 ft (1,600 m)

The deepest known canyons on Earth are the Yarlung Tsangpo and the Kali Gandaki (in Nepal).

Yarlung Tsangpo (Tibet, China)
308 miles (496 km)

Grand Canyon (US)
277 miles (445 km)

Hell's Canyon (US)
125 miles (201 km)

Fish River Canyon (Namibia)
100 miles (160 km)

The longest canyon on Earth, the Yarlung Tsangpo, is also the world's biggest canyon. It was cut through Tibet by the Yarlung Tsangpo River, which becomes the Brahmaputra River when it later flows through India.

Canyons are created by the movement of rivers, weathering, erosion, or tectonic plate movement. Valles Marineris may have started as a huge tectonic "crack" in the planet's crust, later widened by erosion.

Solar system data

How long would it take a plane traveling at 560 mph (900 kph) to **reach each planet** from the Sun?

THE SIZE

OF THE SOLAR SYSTEM is equal to

100,000

times the distance from the Sun to the Earth.

Traveling at 186,282 miles per second (299,792 km per second), sunlight takes

8¼ minutes

to reach Earth from the Sun, and **555.5 days** to reach the edge of the solar system.

A **LONG** DAY

Because Mercury spins very slowly and orbits so close to the Sun, its day (measuring 176 Earth days), is actually

longer

than its year, which lasts for 87.87 Earth days.

COMETS

The nucleus of a comet can range in size from

300 ft to 25 miles

(100 m to 40 km)

Comets formed at the same time as the rest of solar system, around

4.5

billion years ago. Like the planets, comets orbit the Sun.

When a comet gets near the Sun, its nucleus begins to melt, forming a **tail** of gas and dust that can

stretch

for **millions of miles**.

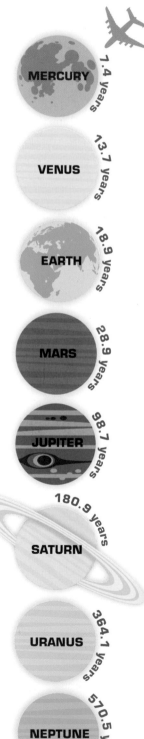

MERCURY 7.4 years
VENUS 13.7 years
EARTH 18.9 years
MARS 28.9 years
JUPITER 98.7 years
SATURN 180.9 years
URANUS 364.1 years
NEPTUNE 570.5 years

DAY LENGTH

A **day** is measured as the **time** it takes for a planet to **spin once on its axis** so that the Sun returns to the same spot in the sky.

Mercury: 176 Earth days
Venus: 117 Earth days
Mars: 24 hr 40 min
Jupiter: 9 hr 56 min
Saturn: 10 hr 33 min
Uranus: 17 hr 14 min
Neptune: 16 hr 6 min

This list measures day length in Earth days, hours, and minutes.

DEEP PROBES

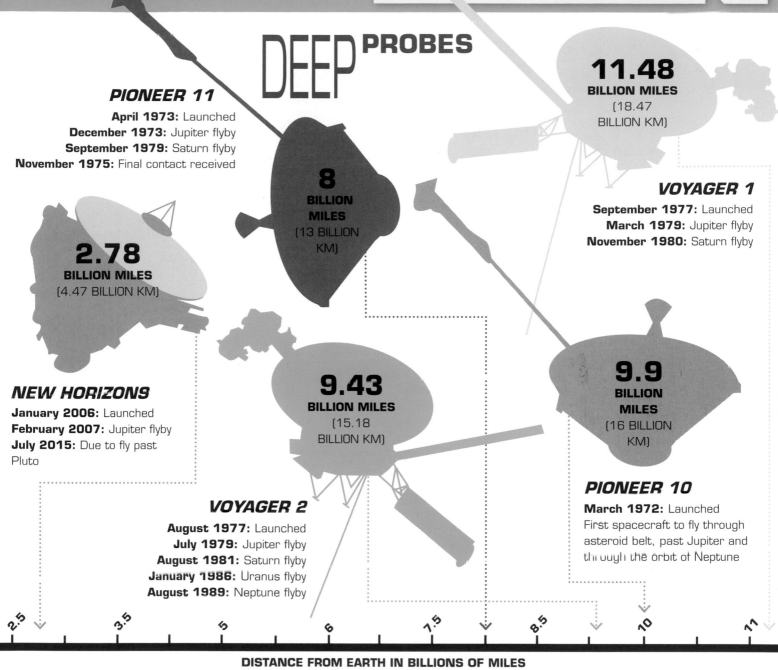

PIONEER 11

April 1973: Launched
December 1973: Jupiter flyby
September 1979: Saturn flyby
November 1975: Final contact received

11.48 BILLION MILES
(18.47 BILLION KM)

8 BILLION MILES
(13 BILLION KM)

VOYAGER 1

September 1977: Launched
March 1979: Jupiter flyby
November 1980: Saturn flyby

2.78 BILLION MILES
(4.47 BILLION KM)

NEW HORIZONS

January 2006: Launched
February 2007: Jupiter flyby
July 2015: Due to fly past Pluto

9.43 BILLION MILES
(15.18 BILLION KM)

9.9 BILLION MILES
(16 BILLION KM)

PIONEER 10

March 1972: Launched
First spacecraft to fly through asteroid belt, past Jupiter and through the orbit of Neptune

VOYAGER 2

August 1977: Launched
July 1979: Jupiter flyby
August 1981: Saturn flyby
January 1986: Uranus flyby
August 1989: Neptune flyby

2.5   3.5   5   6   7.5   8.5   10   11

DISTANCE FROM EARTH IN BILLIONS OF MILES

DWARF PLANETS

In addition to the eight large planets, the solar system is also home to a number of smaller objects known as **dwarf planets**. The biggest discovered so far are:

Eris: radius
723 miles (1,163 km)

Pluto: radius
715 miles (1,151 km)

Makemake: radius
441 miles (710 km)

EXOPLANETS

Ours is not the only solar system. Other stars are also orbited by large satellites known as **exoplanets**.

The exoplanet **HAT-p-32b** is 1,044 light-years from Earth and orbits a Sunlike star. Its **radius** is twice that of Jupiter. However, its **mass** is slightly less than that of Jupiter.

The exoplanet **KO-55.01**, 3,850 light-years from Earth, is **11 times** denser than Earth. It orbits its star, which is one-fifth the size of the Sun, every 5.8 hours—the **shortest orbit** of any known planet.

How **big** is the **biggest star?**

Hypergiant stars can be **hundreds of times** wider than the **Sun**. The **largest known star** is called **VY Canis Majoris**, whose diameter is nearly **1.3 billion miles** (2 billion km).

VY Canis Majoris's diameter is about 1,400 times bigger than the Sun's.

FAST FACTS

If it were in the center of our solar system, VY Canis Majoris would engulf all the inner, rocky planets, including Earth. It would even swallow Jupiter, so the innermost surviving planet would be Saturn! When our own Sun begins to die in 5 billion years, it will swell to become a red giant, growing beyond the present orbit of Earth.

Saturn

Jupiter

Mars

Earth

Sun

VY Canis Majoris

Aldebaran is a red giant star 67 light-years away and 44 times wider than the Sun.

Arcturus is a red giant 37 light-years away and 25 times wider than the Sun. It is the fourth-brightest star in the night sky.

When compared with giant, supergiant, and hypergiant stars, our own Sun appears tiny.

Sun

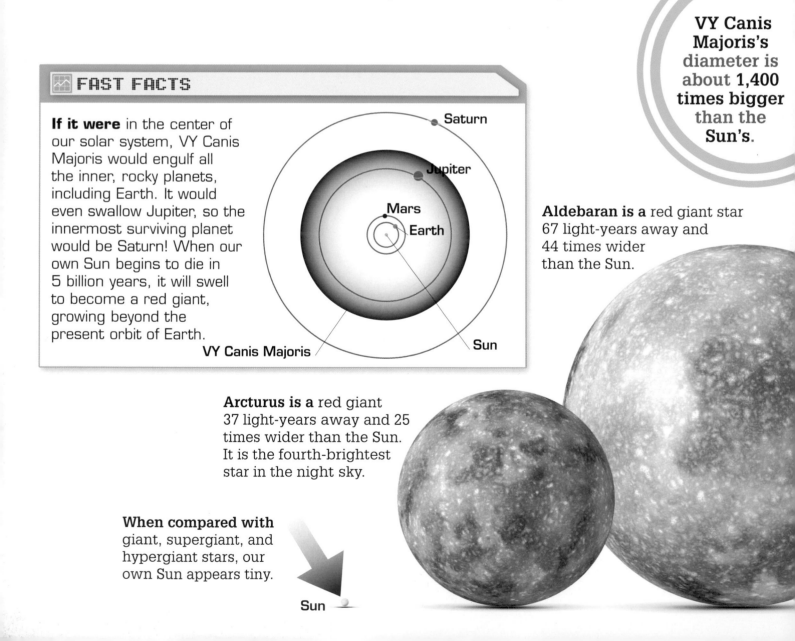

SUPERNOVA

When large red giants die, their cores may collapse under their great gravity, then may explode with incredible force. These explosions are called supernovas, and they blow a star's matter into space as a cloud of dust and gas called a nebula. This one is the Crab Nebula, and it comes from a star that exploded like this in 1054 CE.

VY Canis Majoris is a red hypergiant about 4,000 light-years away. It is 1,400 times wider than the Sun, but only 20–30 times heavier. Its outer layers are very thin—1,000 times thinner than Earth's atmosphere. VY Canis Majoris is burning very brightly, producing about 500,000 times as much light as the Sun. The force of its burning is pushing its thin outer layers out into space.

Rigel is a blue-white supergiant 860 light-years away and around 75 times wider than the Sun. In spite of its distance from Earth, it is so luminous that it is still one of the brightest stars in our sky.

Neutron stars are among the most extreme places in the universe. Their temperature is more than 1.8 million °F (1 million °C) and some spin hundreds of times a second. Gravity on their surface is around 200 billion times stronger than it is on Earth.

Neutron stars appear a dim blue-white color. Because they are so hot, they give off little visible light. Instead of light, they shine with more powerful X-rays.

FAST FACTS

A neutron star is the core of a giant star that has collapsed under its own gravity. The collapse squeezes the neutron star's matter into a minute space.

Earth ⬤ Neutron star

Neutron stars shrink so much when they collapse that they pack a mass greater than the Sun into a sphere less than 12 miles (20 km) in diameter—about the size of a city. A neutron star's diameter is 600 times smaller than the Earth's.

What is the heaviest stuff in the universe?

The **matter** in a **neutron star** is so dense that a piece the size of **sugar cube** weighs the same as all the **humans** on **Earth.**

PULSING STAR

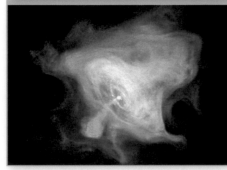

In the center of this whirling disk of hot matter is a neutron star blasting out a beam of radiation and a plume of hot gas. Thirty times every second, the beam points toward Earth, giving viewers a pulse of light.

A pinhead has a volume of around 1 cu mm. The matter in a neutron star is so dense that a pinhead-sized piece would weigh 1.1 million tons (1 million metric tons).

Pinhead-sized piece of neutron star material

A pinhead-sized blob of matter from a neutron star is as heavy as three Empire State Buildings.

The Empire State Building weighs 365,000 tons (331,000 metric tons), so three would weigh 1,095,000 tons (993,000 metric tons).

How fast is light?

It may seem to move instantly, but **light** takes time to get from place to place. In space, **light travels at 671 million mph** (1,080,000,000 kph), or **186,282 miles** (299,792 km) in **1 second**.

An imaginary light beam begins its journey

Stopwatch reads
0 seconds

FAST FACTS

Vacuum 100% speed

Air 99.97% speed

Water 75% speed

Glass 65% speed

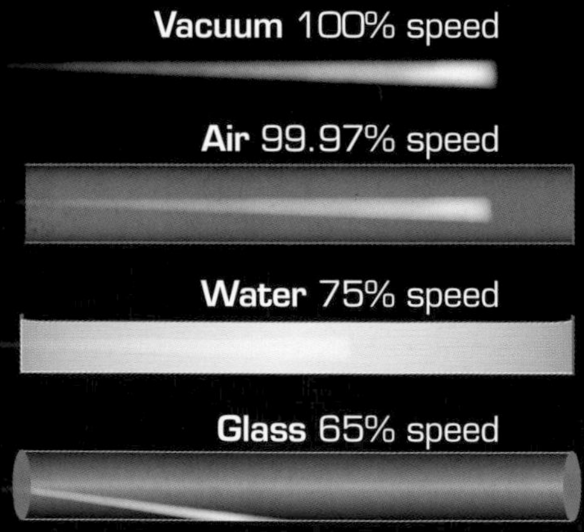

Light travels at a constant speed in a vacuum, but it slows down when there are particles in the way. In air, it travels at 99.97 percent of its speed in a vacuum, in water 75 percent, and in glass about 65 percent.

This picture shows light bending, but in reality, light only curves sharply like this when pulled by really intense gravity, such as that generated by a black hole. Earth's gravity is too weak to make much difference to light's straight-line path.

In just
1 second,
a beam of **light**
would travel
around **Earth**
7.5 times.

LUNAR LASER

A laser beam, traveling at
the speed of light, takes 1.28
seconds to reach the Moon.
From this, we can precisely
measure the distance from
the Earth to the Moon:
238,854 miles (384,399 km).

The light beam completes
its 1-second journey
more than 18,000 times
quicker than the fastest-
ever spacecraft—the *New
Horizons* probe, which
reached (36,373 mph/
58,536 kph) as it left the
Earth's atmosphere in 2006.

Stopwatch reads
1 second

How cold is space?

Temperatures in **outer space** can reach extremes of hot and cold, but the **average temperature,** far from any star, is −454.8°F (−270.4°C).

Sun's surface 9,630°F (5,330°C)

Venus 867°F (464°C)

Mercury 354°F (179°C)

Earth 57°F (14°C)

Pluto −364°F (−230°C)

Average temperatures

The Sun's surface is 9,630°F (5,330°C), but the core tops 27 million °F (15 million °C). Although Mercury is the closest planet to the Sun, Venus's thick atmosphere makes it the hottest.

Water's boiling point, the temperature at which it turns into water vapor, is 212°F (100°C) at sea level.

The freezing point of water, the temperature at which it turns to ice, is 32°F (0°C).

The coldest known temperature on Earth's surface was −128.6°F (−89°C), recorded in 1983 at Vostok, Antarctica.

°C 100 80 60 40 20 0 −20 −40 −60 −80

°F 200 150 100 100 0 −50 −100

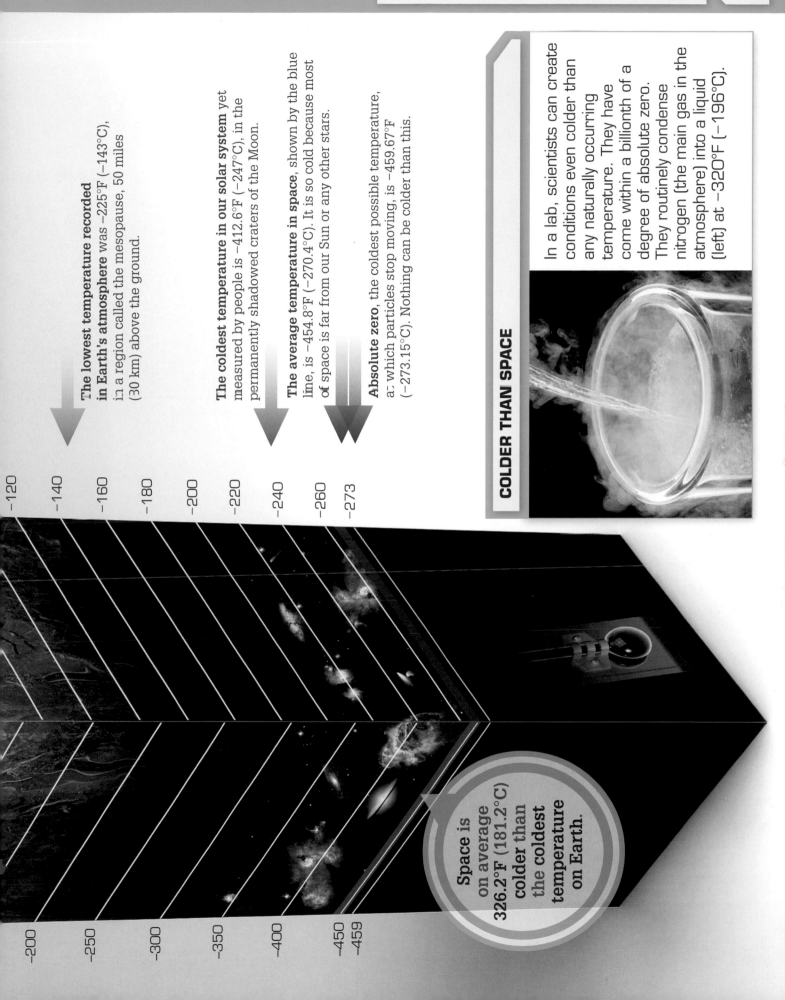

The lowest temperature recorded in Earth's atmosphere was −225°F (−143°C), in a region called the mesopause, 50 miles (30 km) above the ground.

The coldest temperature in our solar system yet measured by people is −412.6°F (−247°C), in the permanently shadowed craters of the Moon.

The average temperature in space, shown by the blue line, is −454.8°F (−270.4°C). It is so cold because most of space is far from our Sun or any other stars.

Absolute zero, the coldest possible temperature, at which particles stop moving, is −459.67°F (−273.15°C). Nothing can be colder than this.

Space is on average 326.2°F (181.2°C) colder than the coldest temperature on Earth.

−120
−140
−160
−180
−200
−220
−240
−260
−273

−200
−250
−300
−350
−400
−450
−459

COLDER THAN SPACE

In a lab, scientists can create conditions even colder than any naturally occurring temperature. They have come within a billionth of a degree of absolute zero. They routinely condense nitrogen (the main gas in the atmosphere) into a liquid (left) at −320°F (−196°C).

How big is the universe?

The **universe** is **unimaginably vast. Distances** are so **huge** that scientists measure them in **light-years**—the distance that light travels in one year.

The Milky Way, a disk-shaped spiral galaxy, contains the solar system. This galaxy is about 100,000 light-years across. One light-year is 5,879 billion miles (9,461 billion km).

FAST FACTS

ONE YEAR

J F M A
M J J A
S O N D

31

The universe is 13.77 billion years old. Humans have not been around for that long. If the universe were just a year old, *Homo sapiens* (humans) would have only emerged at 11:52 p.m. on New Year's Eve.

The Sun is about 93 million miles (150 million km) from planet Earth.

The solar system contains the Sun and the objects traveling around it, which include Earth, seven other planets, and many asteroids.

Our home, Earth, is a small planet measuring about 7,918 miles (12,742 km) across.

From top to bottom, South America stretches about 4,660 miles (7,500 km).

The orbit of Uranus, the solar system's second most distant planet, lies on average `1.78 billion miles (2.87 billion km) from the Sun.

THE MILKY WAY

Although disk-shaped, the Milky Way appears in our skies as a bright band. That's because Earth (and all stars visible without a telescope) sits within the disk.

The Andromeda galaxy is a large galaxy in the Local Group, a cluster of nearly 46 galaxies.

The Local Group of galaxies takes up an area of space that is about 10 million light-years across. The Milky Way is a tiny part of the Local Group.

A supermassive black hole is thought to sit in the middle of the Milky Way. It contains as much mass as 4 million Suns.

The edge of the observable universe is 13.7 billion light-years away.

This image taken by the Hubble Telescope shows galaxies up to 13.7 billion light-years away. However, the universe has expanded since light left these galaxies, so they are now even farther away.

The red dots are the most distant galaxies that we can see.

Universe data

INSIDE A STAR

THE PHOTOSPHERE
The part of the Sun we see from Earth

CORE

CONVECTIVE ZONE
Where energy rises to the surface

RADIATIVE ZONE
Where energy shines outward in the form of light

Stars, such as our Sun, come in many different **types** and **sizes**, but all work in largely the same way. At their

cOre

atomic collisions take place that create **huge amounts of energy**. This **energy** is then **transferred** through the star to its surface and **out into space**.

OLD TIMER

13.8

The universe is believed to be 13.8 billion years old.

GALAXIES

There are four main types of galaxy:

SPIRAL

ELLIPTICAL

LENTICULAR

IRREGULAR

STAR LIFE

How a star **ends its life** depends on its size and mass. When an average Sunlike star begins to run out of fuel, it e**xpands**

AVERAGE SUN-LIKE STAR — **RED GIANT** → **PLANETARY NEBULA**

MASSIVE STAR — **RED SUPERGIANT** → **SUPERNOVA**

to become a cooler, fainter star known as a **red giant**. It eventually sheds its outer layers, forming a cloud of material called a **planetary nebula**. More massive stars become **red supergiants**, which eventually tear themselves apart in gigantic explosions known as **supernovas**.

TRAVELING AT *LIGHT SPEED*

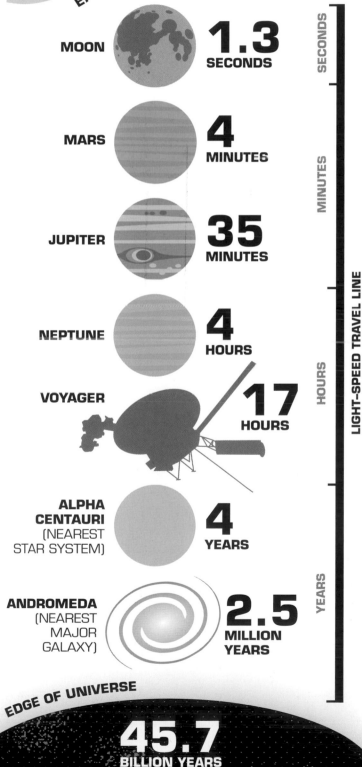

The **speed of light** is the fastest speed there is—**186,282 miles per second** (299,797 km per second). But the universe is so vast that, even traveling at this great speed, it can take a long time to travel around.

EARTH

MOON
1.3
SECONDS

MARS
4
MINUTES

JUPITER
35
MINUTES

NEPTUNE
4
HOURS

VOYAGER
17
HOURS

ALPHA CENTAURI
(NEAREST STAR SYSTEM)
4
YEARS

ANDROMEDA
(NEAREST MAJOR GALAXY)
2.5
MILLION YEARS

SECONDS · MINUTES · HOURS · YEARS

LIGHT-SPEED TRAVEL LINE

EDGE OF UNIVERSE
45.7
BILLION YEARS

THE SUN IN 5 BILLION YEARS TIME

............**THE SUN TODAY**

BIG **SUNS** AND BIG BANGS

When the **Sun dies**, in around **5 billion years' time**, it will **expand** to around **100 times** its current width.

The most **massive** stars burn ferociously quickly and die out in just a few million years. But **smaller** stars, known as **red dwarfs**, can glow weakly for trillions of years. The massive star **Eta Carinae**, located 8,000 light-years from Earth, is due to **explode** as a supernova soon. When it does, it could be the **brightest** object in the sky after the Sun—bright enough to read by at night.

MILKY WAY

Our galaxy, the **Milky Way**, is a spiral around **100,000 light-years** across. It is believed to contain more than **200 billion stars**.

The nearest major galaxy to us, the **Andromeda galaxy**, is about 2.5 million light-years away. It is **260,000 light-years across**—more than twice the size of the Milky Way—and contains around **400 billion stars**.

Astounding Earth

Our planet has been shaped by immense forces since it was formed—from volcanic eruptions and asteroids to the weather. Today, high mountains stretch skyward, canyons and caves plunge into Earth's depths, and vast rivers snake across the land.

Tourists at the Grand Canyon, Arizona, marvel at the view—and the hair-raising drop! The canyon is just over 1 mile (1.8 km) deep—the height of four Empire State Buildings stacked one on top of the other.

Which is the biggest continent?

At **17,207,994 sq miles** (44,568,500 sq km), **Asia** is the **biggest** of the world's seven large landmasses, or **continents**.

Australasia has an area of 3,291,903 sq miles (8,525,989 sq km), and includes Australia, New Zealand, New Guinea, and some of the islands in between.

Europe has an area of 3,840,944 sq miles (9,948,000 sq km) and covers only 7 per cent of the land surface and is only slightly bigger than Canada.

Antarctica covers an area of 5,405,430 sq miles (14,000,000 sq km). This landmass is almost entirely covered in ice.

A continent is usually a large mass of land that is separated from another by water. In fact, five of the seven continents are joined. Europe and Asia are sometimes considered as a single continent, Eurasia.

Asia
covers about
30 percent
of the Earth's
land surface.

South American has an area of 6,879,954 sq miles (17,819,000 sq km). This continent stretches from just above the Equator down to the Antarctic.

North America covers 9,449,078 sq miles (24,473,000 sq km). Greenland is part of this continent, although it belongs to Denmark.

Africa has an area of 11,608,161 sq miles (30,065,000 sq km). It covers an area more than three times bigger than the USA.

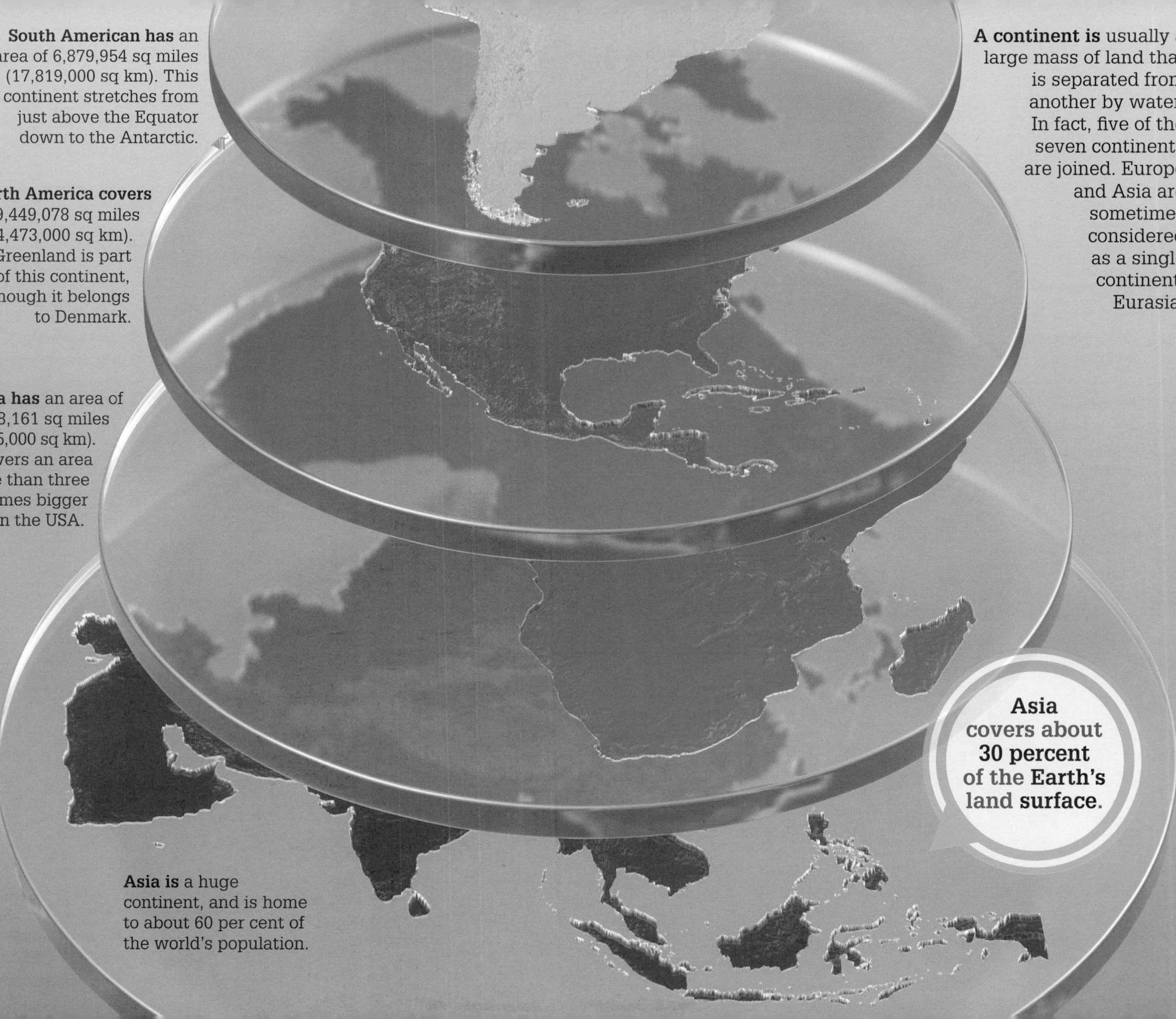

Asia is a huge continent, and is home to about 60 per cent of the world's population.

The distance across France is 605 miles (974 km). A TGV train can cross it in just under four hours.

The distance across Algeria is 1,500 miles (2,400 km). Travel can be tricky due to sand dunes forming on roads in the Sahara.

The distance across Australia is 2,475 miles (3,983 km). The train journey from east to west passes along the world's longest stretch of straight track, which measures 297 miles (478 km).

France

Algeria

Australia

USA

Russia

The distance across the US is 2,807 miles (4,517 km). It would take about 2 months traveling 50 miles (80 km) per day to cycle across it.

The distance across Russia is 5,996 miles (9,650 km). The country is so wide that the eastern edge of the country is nine hours ahead of the west.

SMALLEST COUNTRY

The smallest country in the world is the Vatican City. It occupies 0.17 sq miles (0.44 sq km) within Rome, Italy. That is roughly the area of 65 soccer fields. Fewer than 1,000 people live there.

What is the biggest country?

Russia stretches across **two continents** and covers **11.5 percent** of the **Earth's surface**.

Russia

Russia is nearly twice as wide as the US (excluding Alaska) and nearly 10 times as wide as France.

Vladivostok in Russia is at the eastern end of the Trans-Siberian railroad, which crosses Russia from Moscow. The 5,772-mile (9,289-km) journey takes 6 days.

📊 FAST FACTS

Africa contains more countries than any other continent.

Africa 54
Europe 47
Asia 44
North America 23
Oceania 14
South America 12
Antarctica 0 (It belongs to no one.)

How **big** is the largest lake?

> The water in **all five** of the North American Great Lakes combined **would not fill** Lake Baikal.

NORTH AMERICA'S GREAT LAKES

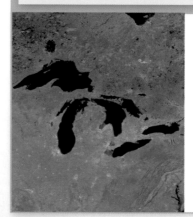

The Great Lakes lie on the Canada–United States border and hold 84 percent of North America's fresh surface water. They were carved out 10,000 years ago by glaciers.

The bed of Lake Baikal is shown here at its average depth of about 2,487 ft (758 m). At its deepest point, however, the lake bed plunges to 5,387 ft (1,642 m) deep.

Lake Baikal

Lake Superior

Lake Ontario

Lake Baikal contains roughly 20 percent of the world's unfrozen fresh surface water.

Lake Superior contains just over half the amount of water of Lake Baikal and is on average 482 ft (147 m) deep. It is the largest of the Great Lakes in terms of area, depth, and volume of water.

Lake Ontario is 282 ft (86 m) deep on average, and Lake Baikal would fill it 15 times.

The **largest freshwater lake** in the world by volume is **Lake Baikal**, in Siberia. It contains around **6,238,500 billion gallons** (23,615,000 billion liters) of water.

FAST FACTS

The Caspian Sea, between Asia and Europe, is 12 times larger than Lake Baikal in area and contains three times as much water. It is salty and is all that remains of an ancient ocean. Experts think of it as an inland sea, rather than a lake.

Lake Balkal

Caspian Sea

Lake Superior

Ligeia Mare

Lake Michigan

Lake Huron

Saturn's moon, Titan, has several huge lakes made of liquid methane. Ligeia Mare is similar in size to one of the Great Lakes. Kraken Mare is even bigger, at around the size of the Caspian Sea.

Together, the Great Lakes cover an area more than seven times greater than that of Lake Baikal. But Lake Baikal holds more water because it is so deep. In fact, it's the deepest lake on Earth, and also the oldest. It was created some 25 million years ago, when Earth's crust pulled apart to create a deep valley, which filled with water.

Lake Michigan

Lake Huron

Lake Erie

Lake Michigan has an average depth of 279 ft (85 m) and contains one-fifth the amount of water in Lake Baikal.

Lake Huron has an average depth of 194 ft (59 m) and one-seventh of the amount of water in Lake Baikal.

Lake Erie is only 62 ft (19 m) deep on average. It would take nearly 50 lakes this size to fill Lake Baikal.

What is the biggest river?

Although not as **long** as the **Nile**, the **Amazon** carries **far more water**. It empties **58 million gallons** (219 million liters) into the ocean every second—that's **one fifth** of all the **world's river water flow.**

Along much of its length, the Amazon is 1–6 miles (1.6–10 km) wide in the dry season. In the rainy season, however, some parts expand to 30 miles (48 km) or more.

Pará River

FAST FACTS

The Amazon Basin is the area drained by the Amazon River. It is almost as big as Australia and is the largest river basin in the world. It covers 40 percent of South America, and all of it recieves heavy yearly rainfall, which swells the river with water.

The Pará River joins the Amazon at its mouth, broadening its estuary still farther.

The Amazon spreads out when it reaches the Atlantic Ocean and merges with the mouth of another wide river, the Pará. This image shows the region around this mouth, or estuary—sometimes called "The Mouths of the Amazon."

More than 1,100 tributaries feed directly into the Amazon, 15 of which are themselves more than 620 miles (1,000 km) long.

FLOODED RAIN FOREST

In the yearly rainy season, the Amazon River rises over 30 ft (9 m) and floods about 90,000 sq miles (240,000 sq km) of surrounding forest.

The Amazon Rain Forest, the world's largest rain forest, surrounds the river. It covers much of Brazil and parts of eight other countries.

Amazon River

London to Paris 214 miles (344 km)

The Amazon flows with such force that it sends a plume of freshwater about 250 miles (400 km) into the Atlantic. It floats on the ocean, so freshwater can be found on the surface even far out of sight of land.

The **mouth of the Amazon is nearly as wide as the** distance from **London to Paris.**

How high is the tallest waterfall?

The **tallest waterfall** in the world, **Angel Falls** in Venezuela is **3,212 ft** (979 m) **in height**. Known locally as **Kerepakupai Merú**, it found fame when US pilot **Jimmy Angel** discovered it in 1933.

Vinnufossen, Norway
2,837 ft (865 m)

Sutherland Falls, New Zealand
1,903 ft (580 m)

Surtherland Falls drops down the almost sheer side of a fjord—a valley carved by a glacier and flooded by the sea.

Victoria Falls, Zambia/Zimbabwe
354 ft (108 m)

Niagara Falls, US/Canada
167 ft (51 m)

The spray can be seen from 30 miles (48 km) away.

VICTORIA FALLS

Victoria Falls forms the largest continuous sheet of falling water in the world, at 1.1 miles (1.7 km) wide and 355 ft (108 m) tall.

**Angel Falls,
Venezuela**
3,212 ft (979 m)

FAST FACTS

Niagara Falls

Olympic
swimming pool

Niagara Falls, on the US–Canadian border, is the world's largest waterfall in terms of water flow. In just 1 second, 740,000 gallons (2.8 million litorc) of watcr gush over the falls—enough to fill an Olympic-sized swimming pool.

In 1901, Ann Taylor became the first person to go over Niagara Falls in a barrel and survive to tell the tale. Of the 14 other people who have intentionally gone over the falls since, five did not survive the experience.

Angel Falls is formed by water tumbling down the side of one of the "tepuis," Venezuela's vertical-sided mountains. Here, it is pictured next to some of the world's other tall and famous waterfalls.

The Empire State Building measures 1,453 ft (443 m) tall.

Angel Falls is **more than twice as tall** as New York's **Empire State Building.**

FAST FACTS

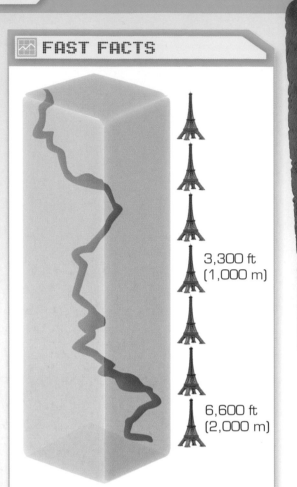

3,300 ft
(1,000 m)

6,600 ft
(2,000 m)

Krubera Cave in Georgia, Eurasia, is the world's deepest at 7,208 ft (2,197 m)—as deep as seven Eiffel Towers.

An underground river runs through the first 1.5 miles (2.5 km) of the 5.5-mile (9-km) cave. There are thought to be more than 150 chambers in total.

How **big** is the **biggest cave?**

Deep in the **Vietnamese jungle** lies the **Hang Son Doong** cave—the **biggest** in the **world.** In places it is more than **650 ft** (200 m) **deep.**

Each of the sinkholes on the surface is up to 330 ft (100 m) across.

Hang Son Doong cave was not discovered until 1991 because it is hidden by thick jungle. The cave formed two to five million years ago, when underground river water eroded away the soluble limestone rock. In places where the limestone was weak, the ceiling collapsed into giant sinkholes.

The Leaning Tower of Pisa would fit inside the deepest shaft six times.

ROCK PILLARS

Stalagmites in the cave, like the "Hand of Dog" shown here, are so big that they make the man standing in the middle look tiny.

The two main chambers within the cave system have 100-ft (30-m) trees growing inside because the roofs fell in and let in enough light for plants to grow.

This shows the upper slopes of Everest. There are deep valleys around the mountain that are not visible here.

Aconcagua, Argentina
22,837 ft (6,961 m)

A mountain's height is usually given as its height above sea level. If you could strip away the land from the base of each mountain and place them together, this is what you would see in terms of height differences.

Mount McKinley, US
20,320 ft (6,194 m)

Mount Kilimanjaro, Tanzania 19,341 ft (5,895 m)

Everest is 10 times taller than the world's tallest building, Dubai's Burj Khalifa.

Mount Everest, Nepal
29,029 ft
(8,848 m)

Burj Khalifa, Dubai
2,717 ft
(828 m)

Sea level

ENDLESS GROWTH

Mount Everest was formed by two tectonic plates (sections of the Earth's crust) colliding. The two plates are still pushing together, so the mountain is growing by about ¼ in (5 mm) every year.

How high is Mount Everest?

The peak of **Mount Everest,** the **highest mountain** in the world, is **29,029 ft (8,848 m)** above sea level.

Mount Elbrus, Russia
18,510 ft (5,642 m)

Vinson Massif, Antarctica
16,077 ft (4,900 m)

Mount Wilhelm, Papua New Guinea
14,793 ft (4,509 m)

These seven mountains are known as the "Seven Summits"; each is the highest mountain on its continent. Reaching the top of all of them has become a mountaineering challenge.

FAST FACTS

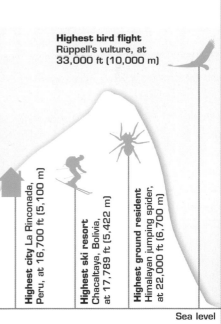

Olympus Mons

Mauna Kea

Everest

Everest is not the Earth's tallest mountain. Measured from its base on the ocean floor, Mauna Kea, Hawaii, is taller. However, both are dwarfed by Olympus Mons on Mars, which is 14 miles (22 km) high.

Highest bird flight
Rüppell's vulture, at 33,000 ft (10,000 m)

Highest city La Rinconada, Peru, at 16,700 ft (5,100 m)

Highest ski resort Chacaltaya, Bolivia, at 17,789 ft (5,422 m)

Highest ground resident Himalayan jumping spider, at 22,000 ft (6,700 m)

Sea level

A small jumping spider on Everest is thought to be the Earth's highest animal ground resident. In Africa, Rüppell's vulture can fly even higher.

⊞ FAST FACTS

The Australian, Arabian, and Sahara deserts are hot deserts in the tropics. The biggest is the Sahara in Africa, which is as big as the US. The Kalahari and Gobi lie farther from the equator and can be cool or even very cold.

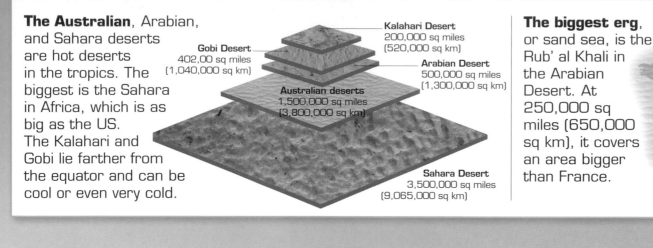

Gobi Desert
402,00 sq miles
(1,040,000 sq km)

Kalahari Desert
200,000 sq miles
(520,000 sq km)

Arabian Desert
500,000 sq miles
(1,300,000 sq km)

Australian deserts
1,500,000 sq miles
(3,800,000 sq km)

Sahara Desert
3,500,000 sq miles
(9,065,000 sq km)

The biggest erg, or sand sea, is the Rub' al Khali in the Arabian Desert. At 250,000 sq miles (650,000 sq km), it covers an area bigger than France.

France

How tall are sand dunes?

Camel trains were the best method of transportation in the Sahara for many centuries and are still sometimes used to carry goods across the desert.

Tall dunes often reach **1,500 ft** (460 m) in height, but occasionally, dunes **can** even **grow** to **4,000 ft** (1,200 m).

MARTIAN SAND DUNES

Near Mars's north pole is a field of dunes covered with frozen pink carbon dioxide in winter. In spring, dark sand trickles down the slopes as the carbon dioxide melts.

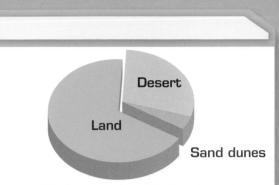

One third of the Earth's land surface is desert, but only 10 percent of the desert is sand dunes. The rest is rock, soil, and sheets of sand.

Desert

Land

Sand dunes

The peak is sculpted Glypha LT Std by winds blowing from many directions, piling sand up into ....

Saharan trader with camel loaded with goods

You could bury the **Eiffel Tower inside a big Saharan star dune.**

This Saharan star dune is 1,500 ft (460 m) tall. Star dunes are pyramid-shaped and they tend to form in areas without a dominant wind direction.

Dust devils are columns of dusty air heated by the Sun. They begin to spin as they rise through the cooler air above. .....

Great Pyramid Original height 481 ft (147 m)

Eiffel Tower 1,052 ft (321 m)

How powerful was the Krakatoa volcano?

In **1883**, Krakatoa, a volcano in **Indonesia**, erupted with a force of about **200 megatons** of **TNT** explosive, or **several nuclear bombs**.

ASH CLOUD LIGHTNING

The electrical charge in the ash cloud from a volcanic eruption can cause lightning, as in the 2010 Eyjafjallajökull eruption in Iceland.

The ash cloud caused by the Krakatoa eruption rose to an estimated height of 50 miles (80 km).

Krakatoa was four times as powerful as the Tsar Bomba, the largest nuclear weapon ever detonated.

The mushroom cloud produced by the detonation of the Tsar Bomba rose to a height of 40 miles (65 km). The bomb was a nuclear weapon dropped over remote Siberian islands during tests by the Soviet Union in 1961.

Krakatoa produced one of the greatest volcanic eruptions in history. It destroyed more than two-thirds of Krakatoa island, killing more than 36,000 people. People reported hearing the explosion 2,800 miles (4,500 km) away.

FAST FACTS

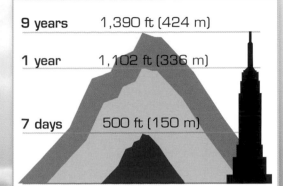

9 years	1,390 ft (424 m)
1 year	1,102 ft (336 m)
7 days	500 ft (150 m)

A volcano in Parícutin, Mexico, suddenly erupted in 1943 from a cornfield. It grew 500 ft (150 m) in one week and continued to erupt and grow for another nine years.

Mt St. Helen's 0.25 cu miles (1 cu km)

Krakatoa 4 cu miles (18 cu km)

Yellowstone 600 cu miles (2,500 cu km)

The Yellowstone supervolcano, 2.1 million years ago, produced 135 times more ash than Krakatoa and 2,500 times more than Mount St. Helen's.

■ Island Park Caldera
■ Tokyo

Yellowstone's Island Park Caldera, an enormous volcanic crater, could fit a city of 13 million people, such as Tokyo, inside it.

What's the largest crater on Earth?

Asteroid and **comet** impacts make **craters** on **Earth** just like they do on the Moon. The **largest** one is the **Vredefort crater** in South Africa, which is over **186 miles** (300 km) **wide.**

You could fit **250 Barringer** craters into Vredefort.

Barringer crater is a well-preserved impact crater in Arizona. Its shape is so clear because it is only 50,000 years old.

Asteroids and comets have battered Earth over the course of its life, but we can see only a few clear craters on Earth's surface today. This is because most craters are worn down or buried under younger rock.

FAST FACTS

Herschel crater
central peak
21,300 ft
(6,500 m)

Mt. Everest
29,029 ft
(8,848 m)

Saturn's moon Mimas is marked by a huge crater, named Herschel, with a central peak made by the shock wave of the impact. The peak is almost as tall as Mount Everest.

The Borealis Basin on Mars is thought to be the biggest known land feature caused by an impact. If it is, it must have been the result of a blow from an object the size of Pluto. The basin covers most of the northern half of Mars, and is nearly five times the size of the US.

US

Borealis Basin

Barringer crater is only ³/₄ mile (1.2 km) in diameter.

Chicxulub crater in Mexico is 110 miles (180 km) wide. It was formed 65 million years ago by the impact of an object 6 miles (10 km) across hitting Earth. The destruction it caused is blamed for the death of the dinosaurs. The crater is now buried and half of it is hidden on the seabed.

Vredefort crater was made around 2 billion years ago. In all that time, it has been eroded by wind, rain, and rivers, and bent and distorted by movements in the Earth's crust.

BIGGEST METEORITE

When an object falls from space and survives the impact, it is known as a meteorite. The Hoba meteorite in Namibia is the biggest ever found and weighs more than 66 tonnes (60 metric tons).

How **big** are the **biggest crystals?**

Crystals of **selenite** discovered in a cave in Mexico measure up to **37 ft 5 in (11.4 m) long.**

With temperatures in the cave of 118 °F (48 °C) and 98 percent humidity, people have to wear protective suits to explore the amazing crystals formations.

 FAST FACTS

The longest Naica crystal found so far, Crystal Cin, is around the length of a bus and weighs about the same as 8 African elephants!

Crystal Cin

Length 37 ft 5 in (11.4 m)

Single decker bus

The oldest crystal in the cave dates back 600,000 years—about the time when *Homo heidelbergensis*, the ancestors of modern humans, first appeared.

Present day

600,000 years ago

These vast selenite crystals are in the Cave of Crystals, which lies 985 ft (300 m) below ground in a mine at Naica, northern Mexico. Selenite is a form of the mineral gypsum. The crystals began to grow because of water boiling in this underground chamber. The water actually boiled for about 500,000 years, the heat solidifying the crystals in the water.

DESERT ROSE

Fingal's Cave, off the coast of Scotland, is unique. It is formed from hexagonal pillars of basalt rock more than 65 ft (20 m) tall. They formed when an ancient lava flow cooled and cracked.

The largest crystals in the cave are more than six times taller than a person.

How much water is there?

The world contains **332 million cu miles** (1.3 billion cu km) of **water** in its oceans, rivers, lakes, groundwater, and clouds, and—as **ice**—in its glaciers and ice caps.

Scooped up, **the world's water** would form **a ball just 860 miles (1,384 km) wide.**

ICE CAPS AND GLACIERS

Only 2.5 percent of the world's water is fresh, and most freshwater is locked up in glaciers and ice caps. Less than 1 percent of the Earth's water is liquid and fresh.

This globe shows the ocean basins with all their water removed. Nearly 97 percent of the world's water is in oceans. The next biggest store of water is the ice caps and glaciers, with 1.75 percent.

Permafrost (underground ice) in Siberia locks up a lot of water. Permafrost and liquid groundwater (water in rocks and soil) make up 1.7 percent of the world's total water.

When water fills this ocean basin, the seabed is around 12,000 ft (4,000 m) below the surface.

FAST FACTS

More than two-thirds of the planet's surface is covered with water, leaving 29 percent land.

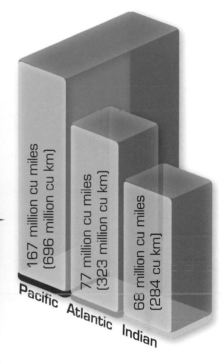

167 million cu miles (696 million cu km)

77 million cu miles (323 million cu km)

68 million cu miles (284 cu km)

Pacific   Atlantic   Indian

The Pacific Ocean contains more water than all the world's other seas and oceans together.

For every tubful of seawater on Earth, there are just 4 teaspoons of freshwater in lakes, rivers, and the atmosphere.

How deep is the ocean?

The **average depth** of the ocean is 14,000 ft (4,300 m), but the **deepest point** is **36,200 ft** (11,030 ft) below sea level at **Challenger Deep** in the Pacific Ocean.

Continental shelves are the shallow regions fringing deep oceans. They are actually part of the continental landmass. A shelf may extend hundreds of miles from the coast.

DEEP-SEA SPOOKFISH

This barreleye, or spookfish, is one of the many peculiar creatures that inhabit the dark ocean depths. The barreleye lives 2,000–2,600 ft (600–800 m) under water and has unique tube-shaped eyes inside a transparent head.

It would take **29 stacked Empire State Buildings to** reach the bottom of **Challenger Deep.**

Continental shelf
Shoreline to 460 ft (140 m)

Continental slope
460–10,500 ft
(140–3,200 m)

Abyssal plain
10,500–20,000 ft
(3,200–6,000 m)

Ocean trench
20,000–36,200 ft
(6,000–11,030 m)

Challenger Deep
36,200 ft (11,030 m)

FAST FACTS

Unexplored ocean

Explored ocean

Humans have explored less than 10 percent of the ocean. Fewer people have traveled to the deepest parts of the ocean than have gone into outer space.

Mount
Everest

Mariana
Trench

The Mariana Trench is about 7 miles (11 km) deep. If Mount Everest were put at the bottom of the trench, the peak would still be more than 1.2 miles (2 km) below sea level.

Cup before dive

Cup after dive

If a polystyrene cup were taken 2 miles (3 km) under water, the pressure at this depth would squeeze it to less than half of its original size.

The seabed is not flat. It starts with a gradual descent down a continental shelf, where the land gives way to sea along the coast. It then plunges down the continental slope to the deep ocean floor, or abyssal plain. The seabed has ridges or deep trenches, such as the Mariana Trench in the western Pacific—where Challenger Deep is located.

How **tall** was the **biggest wave** ever **surfed?**

In 2013, American professional big wave surfer **Garrett McNamara** surfed a **wave** said to be **100 ft** (30 m) **tall** off the coast of Nazaré, Portugal.

FAST FACTS

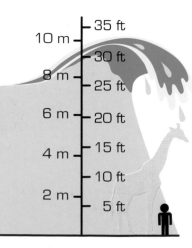

35 ft
10 m
30 ft
8 m
25 ft
6 m
20 ft
4 m
15 ft
10 ft
2 m
5 ft

Tsunamis tend to be less than 33 ft (10 m) tall, but because there is a lot of water following behind them, they cause a flood that reaches far inland. They are caused by earthquakes on the sea bed, land slips, and asteroid strikes.

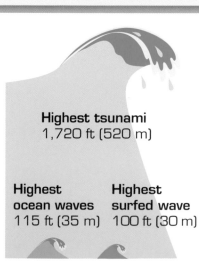

Highest tsunami
1,720 ft (520 m)

Highest ocean waves
115 ft (35 m)

Highest surfed wave
100 ft (30 m)

The biggest wave ever known occurred in Lituya Bay, Alaska, when a slab of rock slipped into the bay and caused a huge tsunami. Giant ocean waves also form far out at sea, caused by high winds and strong currents.

Foaming breakers rise up almost vertically before curling over to form a tube. The surfer tries to stay inside the tube and, if possible, reach the end of it before the wave collapses.

A **100-ft (30-m) wave** is the **height** of nearly **17 people** standing on top of each other.

Surfboards come in a variety of sizes. This championship board is 7 ft (2.1 m) long.

TSUNAMI DAMAGE

Tsunamis are so powerful that anything in their way is flattened and swept away. Even large ships can be carried inland, leaving them stranded miles from the shore.

Record waves occur off Nazaré because it faces the huge swells caused by distant Atlantic storms. An undersea canyon then funnels the wave energy of the swells onto a short stretch of the coast, piling the waters high.

How big was the biggest iceberg?

The **biggest-ever** iceberg began its life when it broke free from an ice shelf off **Antarctica** in 1956. It was **208 miles** (335 km) **long** and **60 miles** (100 km) **wide.**

The biggest iceberg was not really shaped like Belgium. It was longer and thinner, but its area of 12,000 sq miles (31,000 sq km) was slightly larger than Belgium's. It was larger even than iceberg B-15—the Jamaica-sized iceberg that broke off Antarctica's Ross Ice Shelf in 2000.

Antwerp

Brussels

Ghent

Bruges

B E L G

Flanders

HIDDEN DEPTHS

Icebergs float low in the water, with around 90 percent of their height hidden beneath the waves. The ice below the water melts faster than that above it, so that an iceberg may suddenly roll over with a great crash that can be heard for miles.

The biggest-ever iceberg covered an area larger than that of Belgium.

Belgium covers an area of 11,787 sq miles (30,528 sq km), which is about the same size as Maryland.

Liege

I U M

Charleroi

Ardennes

The height of this iceberg is exaggerated in this picture. It would have stood no more than 500 ft (150 m) above the sea's surface.

FAST FACTS

Glacier

Snail

Glaciers are rivers of ice that move very slowly, averaging only 12 in (30 cm) a day. A fast snail can zip across this distance in 2¼ minutes.

Volume of ice today

Volume of ice during the Ice Age

In the last ice age, ice covered more than 30 percent of the planet. Nearly 60 percent of it has melted since then, leaving us with ice only on mountaintops and in the ice caps at the poles.

Tallest iceberg 550 ft (168 m)

Great Pyramid 482 ft (147 m)

The tallest iceberg was sighted near Greenland in 1957. Standing even higher above sea level than the Great Pyramid, the iceberg may have extended another 4,900 ft (1,500 m) below the surface.

What if all the ice melted?

Ten percent of the **world's land** is covered by thick **glaciers** and **ice sheets**. If it all melted, the **sea level** would rise by up to **230 ft** (70 m). Many **major world cities** would be **covered** by the **ocean.**

SHRINKING GLACIERS

Glaciers are great rivers of slowly flowing ice. The ice builds up over many years from fallen snow. Glaciers can begin on any high ground where the snow does not thaw completely in spring. In parts of the Arctic, glaciers reach down to the sea, but most are shrinking. Between 1941 and 2004, the Muir Glacier in Alaska (above) retreated more than 7 miles (12 km) and the sea filled its valley.

Low-lying cities by the coast would be devastated by big sea level rises. New York City would be almost completely swallowed by the ocean, along with the bases of its famous landmarks.

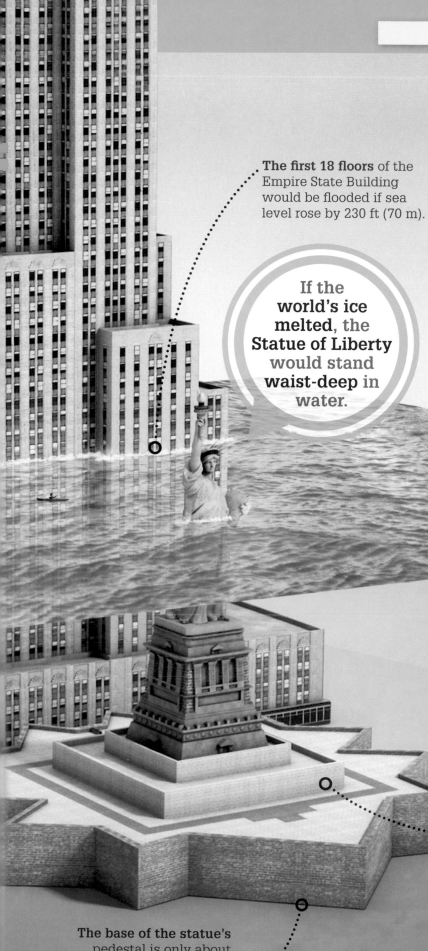

The first 18 floors of the Empire State Building would be flooded if sea level rose by 230 ft (70 m).

If the world's ice melted, the Statue of Liberty would stand waist-deep in water.

The base of the statue's pedestal is only about 20 ft (6 m) above current sea level.

FAST FACTS

Current coastline

Coastline after flooding

If all the ice melted, the coastlines of many countries would dramatically change. Britain and Ireland would turn into a group of smaller islands. Low-lying Bangladesh and the Netherlands would almost disappear.

The ice over Antarctica is extremely thick, averaging 6,000 ft (1,830 m)—nearly as deep as six Eiffel Towers. In some places it is more than twice as deep, at 15,670 ft (4,776 m)

The Statue of Liberty's pedestal is 154 ft (47 m) high.

Earth data

The world's **longest** river is the **Nile**, but the **Amazon** is by far the **largest**. At its mouth in the Atlantic Ocean, it **carries more water** than the next four rivers combined.

L O N G E S T **RIVERS**

RIVER	CONTINENT	LENGTH
NILE	AFRICA	4,145 MILES (6,670 KM)
AMAZON	SOUTH AMERICA	4,000 MILES (6,404 KM)
YANGTZE	ASIA	3,693 MILES (6,378 KM)
MISSISSIPPI-MISSOURI	NORTH AMERICA	3,741 MILES (6,021 KM)
YENISEI-ANGARA	ASIA	3,442 MILES (5,540 KM)

CHANGING CONTINENTS

Earth's crust is divided into **giant** slabs of rock called **tectonic plates**. These plates are moving constantly, but very slowly. Around **200 million years ago**, all the continents were joined into one giant landmass called **Pangea**. The movement of the tectonic plates gradually **broke the continents apart** to form the Earth we know today.

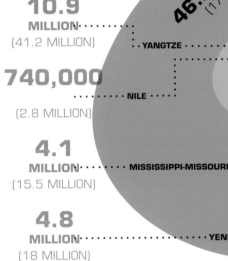

FLOW RATE IN GALLONS (LITERS) PER SECOND

AMAZON 46.2 MILLION (175 MILLION)

10.9 MILLION (41.2 MILLION) · · · · · YANGTZE

740,000 (2.8 MILLION) · · · · · NILE

4.1 MILLION (15.5 MILLION) · · · · MISSISSIPPI-MISSOURI

4.8 MILLION (18 MILLION) · · · · · YENISEI-ANGARA

THE **BIG** ONES

There are **14 mountains** over **26,000 ft** (8,000 m) high. All are found in **Asia** in the region where the Indian subcontinent is pushing into the Asian continent. In 1986, **Reinhold Messner** became the **first mountaineer to climb all 14 peaks**.

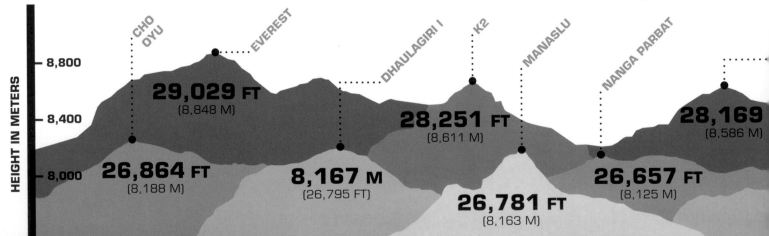

HEIGHT IN METERS

CHO OYU — 26,864 FT (8,188 M)

EVEREST — 29,029 FT (8,848 M)

DHAULAGIRI I — 8,167 M (26,795 FT)

K2 — 28,251 FT (8,611 M)

MANASLU — 26,781 FT (8,163 M)

NANGA PARBAT — 26,657 FT (8,125 M)

— 28,169 (8,586 M)

- 8,800
- 8,400
- 8,000

INSIDE **EARTH**

Our planet is divided into several different **layers**, which get **hotter** the **deeper** you go. The **crust**, where we live, makes up just **0.4%** of Earth's mass.

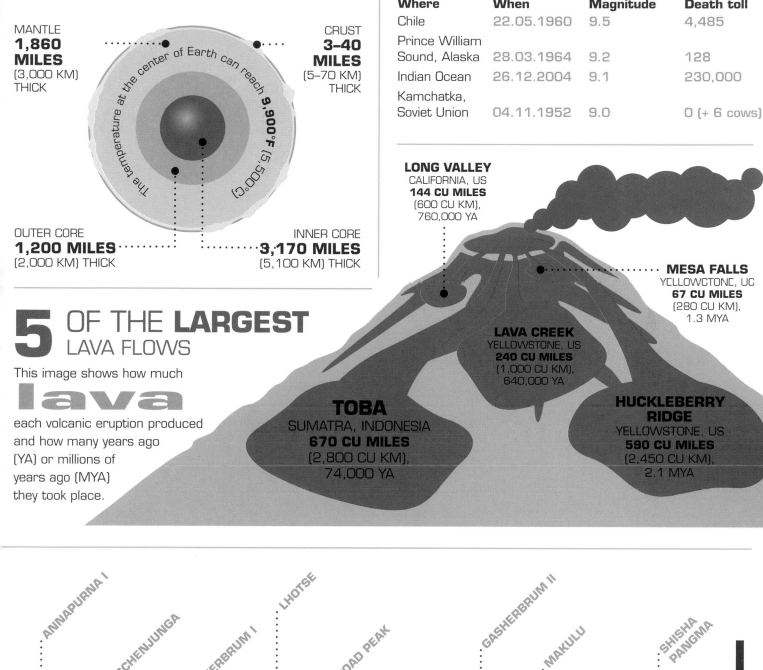

MANTLE
1,860 MILES
(3,000 KM) THICK

CRUST
3–40 MILES
(5–70 KM) THICK

The temperature at the center of Earth can reach **9,900°F (5,500°C)**.

OUTER CORE
1,200 MILES
(2,000 KM) THICK

INNER CORE
3,170 MILES
(5,100 KM) THICK

5 OF THE **LARGEST** LAVA FLOWS

This image shows how much **lava** each volcanic eruption produced and how many years ago (YA) or millions of years ago (MYA) they took place.

LONG VALLEY
CALIFORNIA, US
144 CU MILES
(600 CU KM),
760,000 YA

MESA FALLS
YELLOWSTONE, US
67 CU MILES
(280 CU KM),
1.3 MYA

LAVA CREEK
YELLOWSTONE, US
240 CU MILES
(1,000 CU KM),
640,000 YA

TOBA
SUMATRA, INDONESIA
670 CU MILES
(2,800 CU KM),
74,000 YA

HUCKLEBERRY RIDGE
YELLOWSTONE, US
590 CU MILES
(2,450 CU KM),
2.1 MYA

MOST POWERFUL **EARTHQUAKES**

Where	When	Magnitude	Death toll
Chile	22.05.1960	9.5	4,485
Prince William Sound, Alaska	28.03.1964	9.2	128
Indian Ocean	26.12.2004	9.1	230,000
Kamchatka, Soviet Union	04.11.1952	9.0	0 (+ 6 cows)

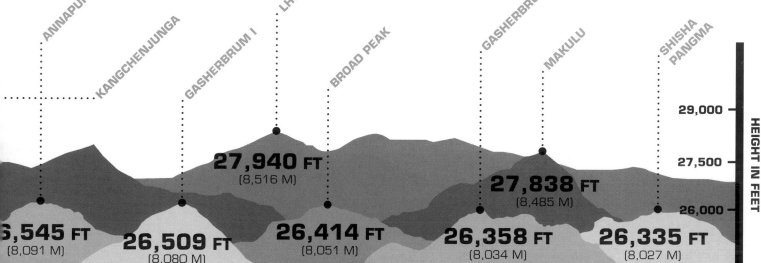

ANNAPURNA I

KANGCHENJUNGA

GASHERBRUM I

LHOTSE

BROAD PEAK

GASHERBRUM II

MAKULU

SHISHA PANGMA

27,940 FT
(8,516 M)

27,838 FT
(8,485 M)

,545 FT
(8,091 M)

26,509 FT
(8,080 M)

26,414 FT
(8,051 M)

26,358 FT
(8,034 M)

26,335 FT
(8,027 M)

HEIGHT IN FEET

29,000

27,500

26,000

Where is the snowiest place on Earth?

The **greatest snowfall** over one year was **95 ft** (29.86 m) in **Mount Baker Ski Area,** Washington, measured in the **1998–1999** season.

Mount Baker's record snowfall **would bury over half the Leaning Tower of Pisa.**

EXTREME SNOW

Japan's sightseeing road, the Tateyama Kurobe Alpine Route, is closed all winter. It opens in spring, when diggers cut through 66 ft (20 m) of snow to the road below.

The Leaning Tower of Pisa is 183 ft 4 in (55.9 m) from the ground on its higher side.

This 100-ft (30-m) pile of snow is much less dense than water. To compare it to a rainfall total, experts would melt it down in a snow gauge, which would produce just 8 ft (2.5 m) of water.

The most snowfall in one month was in Tamarac, California, where 37 ft 5 in (11.4 m) of snow fell in March 1911.

New York City receives an average of 2 ft 5 in (68 cm) of snow every year.

FAST FACTS

Compared to snowfall records, extremes of rainfall are far higher in terms of total amount of water.

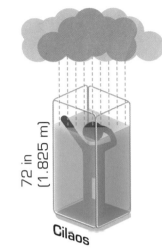

72 in (1.825 m)

Cilaos

The highest-ever rainfall in 24 hours took place in January 1966 in Foc-Foc, on the island of Réunion, where 6 ft (1.825 m) of rain fell.

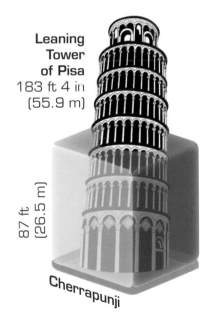

Leaning Tower of Pisa 183 ft 4 in (55.9 m)

87 ft (26.5 m)

Cherrapunji

Cherrapunji, India, saw the most rainfall in one year in 1860–1861, when 87 ft (26.5 m) of rain fell—enough to flood almost half The leaning Tower of Pisa.

How big was the largest hailstone?

The **largest hailstone** ever known fell in **Vivian, South Dakota**, in a storm on **July 23, 2010.** It was **8 in (20 cm)** across.

BISSECTED HAIL

This hailstone cut in half shows the layers of ice that form hail. Hailstones grow because winds in storm clouds throw them upward again and again. Each time, water freezes on to them, building up another layer of ice.

Giant hailstones like this form in clouds with very powerful updrafts, such as those in intense thunderstorms and tornadoes. When giant hail is finally heavy enough to fall to the ground, it can dent cars, smash windshields, flatten crops, and injure living things.

The
South Dakota
hailstone was
about **three times**
the **width** of a
tennis ball.

FAST FACTS

Hail most often forms in giant thunderclouds, which are also the source of lightning.

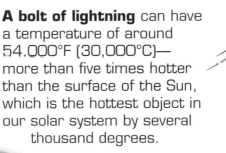

Cloud top
40,000 ft (12,000 m)

Mount Everest
29,029 ft (8,848 m)

Cloud base
6,600 ft (2,000 m)

Thunderclouds, technically known as cumulonimbus, are the tallest kind of clouds. They are sometimes more than 40,000 ft (12,000 m) high—half again as high as the highest mountain. They are column-shaped with a wide, flat top.

A bolt of lightning can have a temperature of around 54,000°F (30,000°C)—more than five times hotter than the surface of the Sun, which is the hottest object in our solar system by several thousand degrees.

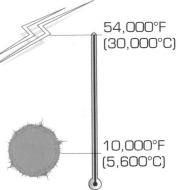

54,000°F
(30,000°C)

10,000°F
(5,600°C)

The lumps that covered the hailstone are the result of smaller hailstones colliding with each other and sticking together. Each lump is a former smaller hailstone with layers of ice added on top

Record hailstone
8 in (20 cm) across,
2 lb 3 oz (1 kg) in weight

Tennis ball
2¾ in (6.7 cm)
across

Weather data

HOT

The **hottest** temperature ever recorded at ground level in the shade was in **Death Valley, California**, in 1913—a scorching

134°F
(56.6°C).

AND COLD

The **coldest** temperature ever recorded at ground level was at **Vostok, Antarctica**, in 1983. It was a bone-chilling

–129°F (–89.2°C).

CLOUD COVER

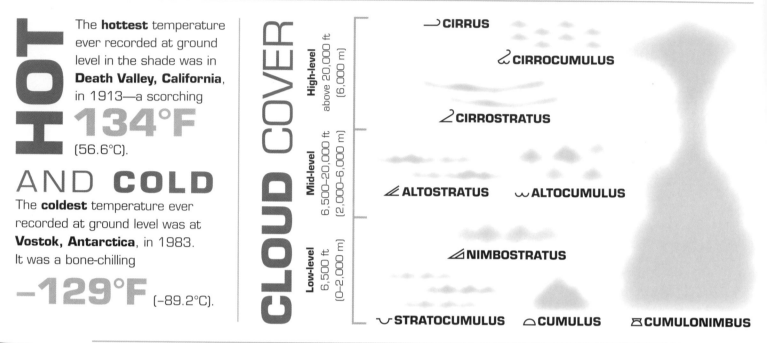

High-level above 20,000 ft (6,000 m)

CIRRUS

CIRROCUMULUS

CIRROSTRATUS

Mid-level 6,500–20,000 ft (2,000–6,000 m)

ALTOSTRATUS   ALTOCUMULUS

Low-level 6,500 ft (0–2,000 m)

NIMBOSTRATUS

STRATOCUMULUS   CUMULUS   CUMULONIMBUS

THE ATMOSPHERE

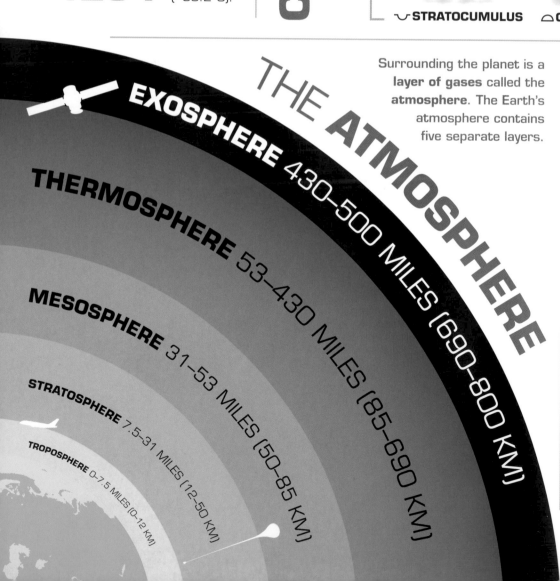

Surrounding the planet is a **layer of gases** called the **atmosphere**. The Earth's atmosphere contains five separate layers.

EXOSPHERE 430–500 MILES (690–800 KM)

THERMOSPHERE 53–430 MILES (85–690 KM)

MESOSPHERE 31–53 MILES (50–85 KM)

STRATOSPHERE 7.5–31 MILES (12–50 KM)

TROPOSPHERE 0–7.5 MILES (0–12 KM)

RAINY DAYS

The **wettest** place on Earth is Mawsynram in northeast India, with average annual rainfall of

467 in
(11,870 mm) per year.

The place with the **most rainy days** each year is Mt. Waialeale, Kauai, Hawaii, with **350** rainy days a year. On average it is dry just one day a month.

The longest continuous rainfall lasted **247 days**, from August 27, 1993, to April 30, 1994, in Kaneohe Ranch, Oahu, Hawaii.

WINDY DAYS

The Beaufort scale lists the effects of increasing wind speeds.

BEAUFORT NUMBER	WIND SPEED	WIND EFFECT ON LAND
0	0	Smoke rises vertically
1	1–2 mph (1–3 kph)	Smoke drifts gently
2	3–7 mph (4–11 kph)	Leaves rustle
3	8–12 mph (12–19 kph)	Twigs move
4	13–18 mph (20–29 kph)	Small branches move
5	19–24 mph (30–39 kph)	Small trees sway
6	25–31 mph (40–50 kph)	Umbrellas hard to use
7	32–38 mph (51–61 kph)	Whole trees sway
8	39–46 mph (62–74 kph)	Difficulty walking
9	47–54 mph (75–87 kph)	Roofs damaged
10	55–63 mph (88–101 kph)	Trees blown down
11	64–74 mph (102–119 kph)	Houses damaged
12	over 74 mph (119 kph)	Buildings destroyed

TWISTERS
300

At ground level, tornadoes have the *fastest winds.* The most powerful recorded had wind speeds of 300 mph (500 kph) or more. Tornadoes can also move at speeds of up to 70 mph (110 kph)—far too fast for anyone to outrun.

HURRICANE DAMAGE

Hurricanes are categorized according to their speed and destructiveness using the Saffir-Simpson scale.

CATEGORY 1

WIND SPEED
74–95 mph
(120–153 kph)

EFFECTS
Minor building damage; branches snapped

CATEGORY 2

96–110 mph
(154–177 kph)

Some roof, door, and window damage

CATEGORY 3

111–130 mph
(178–208 kph)

Roof tiles dislodged; large trees uprooted

CATEGORY 4

131–155 mph
(209–251 kph)

Roofs blown off; major coastal flooding

CATEGORY 5

over 155 mph
(over 252 kph)

Buildings destroyed; catastrophic flooding

BOLTS FROM THE BLUE

Lightning strikes somewhere on Earth **100** times a second. It strikes the Empire State Building roughly **100** times a year.

What was the biggest natural disaster ?

The **disease** known as the **Black Death**, which swept the world in the 14th century, **killed** up to **75 million people**.

The Rose Bowl sports stadium, Pasadena, California, USA, has an official capacity of about 91,000 people.

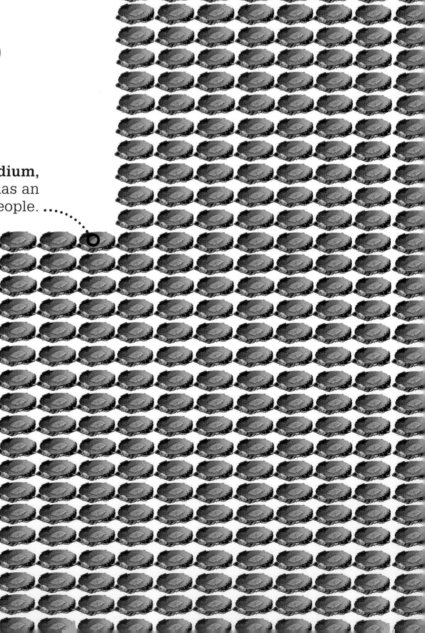

SPANISH FLU

In 1918, after World War I, there was a global outbreak of the disease "Spanish Flu." Spread by the mass movement of troops, it killed over 50 million people—more than the war itself. Diseases on a global scale are called pandemics.

The Black Death, or plague, was caused by bacteria carried by fleas on rats. It began in Central Asia but spread quickly, as rats boarded merchant ships, taking the disease with them. The plague reached Europe in 1346, where it killed up to 60 percent of the population.

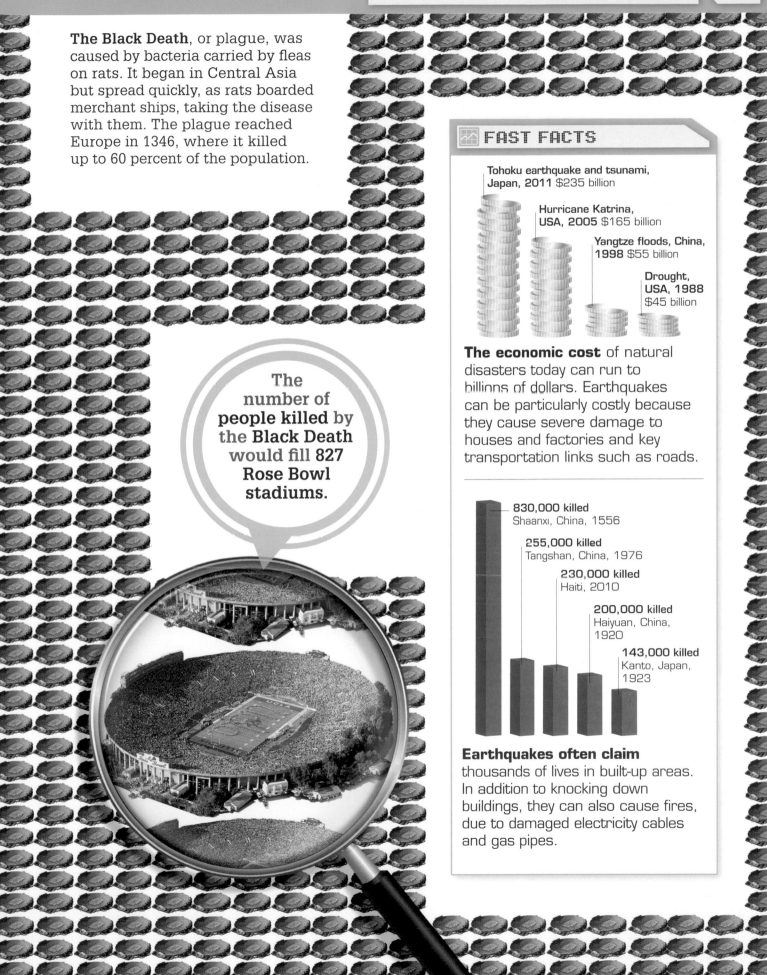

The number of **people killed** by the **Black Death** would fill 827 **Rose Bowl** stadiums.

FAST FACTS

Tohoku earthquake and tsunami, Japan, **2011** $235 billion

Hurricane Katrina, USA, **2005** $165 billion

Yangtze floods, China, **1998** $55 billion

Drought, USA, **1988** $45 billion

The economic cost of natural disasters today can run to billions of dollars. Earthquakes can be particularly costly because they cause severe damage to houses and factories and key transportation links such as roads.

830,000 killed
Shaanxi, China, 1556

255,000 killed
Tangshan, China, 1976

230,000 killed
Haiti, 2010

200,000 killed
Haiyuan, China, 1920

143,000 killed
Kanto, Japan, 1923

Earthquakes often claim thousands of lives in built-up areas. In addition to knocking down buildings, they can also cause fires, due to damaged electricity cables and gas pipes.

How many people are there in China?

The **population** of **China**, including Taiwan, is about **1.4 billion**. In around 2050, **India** is likely to displace China as the world's most populous country.

Australia is the world's sixth-largest country, after Russia, Canada, China, the US, and Brazil.

Australia

China

CHINESE COMMUNITIES

One in every five people on Earth is Chinese. Most major cities outside of China have large Chinese communities, making Chinese culture an important influence actoss the world.

There are as many people in China today as there were in the whole world around 150 years ago!

The area of China is only slightly greater than that of the US, and Australia is not far behind. But China's population is more than four times bigger than the US's and about 60 times larger than that of Australia. Here, the three countries are shown in proportion to their populations.

China has a population 60 times larger than that of **Australia**.

United States

The US has about 316 million people—nearly 14 times more than live in Australia.

Australia
Population of about 23 million
Density of 9 people per sq mile

Sri Lanka
Population of about 21 million
Density of 900 people per sq mile

Australia and Sri Lanka have roughly similar-sized populations, but Australia is about 120 times larger. If Australia were as densely populated as Sri Lanka, it would be home to nearly 2.5 billion people!

Manila, Philippines

London, UK

Court area
2,808 sq ft
(261 sq m)

Some cities are more crowded than others. If Manila and London were divided into tennis courts, Manila would have 11 people on each court and London only one.

How **fast** is the **population** of the world **growing**?

Around **360,000 babies** are **born each day** and about **160,000 people die**. So overall, the world's population **grows by 200,000 people** every **day** of the year.

AGING WORLD

The world's population is getting older. Better health care means that more babies are surviving, and so people are having fewer children. It also enables older people to live longer.

At least another two people would be added to the crowd every second.

FAST FACTS

The human population is growing faster in some places than in others. Using a graph called a population pyramid, we can see which countries have fast-growing populations.

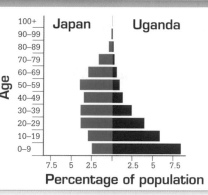

Japan   Uganda

Age

100+
90–99
80–89
70–79
60–69
50–59
40–49
30–39
20–29
10–19
0–9

7.5   5   2.5   2.5   5   7.5

Percentage of population

Japan's narrow-based, bulging pyramid shows an older population, with relatively few young people. The birth rate is low and the population is falling.

Uganda's sloping pyramid shows the country has a high birth rate, many children but few older people, and a fast-growing population.

This crowd of 8,000 people shows how much Earth's population increases every single hour.

In just one hour, the world's population grows by more than 8,000 people. That's the same as 23 plane-loads of passengers arriving on the planet every 60 minutes. Over one day, there would be enough new inhabitants of Earth to fill London's Olympic Stadium 2.5 times.

Humans and other life-forms

Earth is rich in wonderful life-forms—including us! Our bodies perform fantastic feats each day just to keep us alive. We share our world with a host of other incredible plants and animals—some massive, others tiny—many of which have extraordinary abilities.

The manta ray is a gentle giant that "flies" through the water by beating its huge winglike fins. Mantas can grow up to 23 ft (7 m) wide—the same as the average height of 3.5 men. They can weigh up to 3,000 lb (1,350 kg)—the equivalent of two adult cows.

How much blood does a heart pump?

Oxygen-poor **blood** returns to the heart through veins (shown in blue).

The average **adult human heart** pumps about **8¾ pints** (5 liters) of blood **every minute**, which is the **total amount** of blood in a **man's body.**

EXTREME PHYSIQUES

When cyclist Miguel Indurain won five Tours de France in the 1990s, his heart could pump 88 pints (50 liters) of blood a minute and his lungs could hold 14 pints (8 liters) of air. Average adult lungs hold less than 10½ pints (6 liters).

The muscle that makes up the wall of the heart has its own blood supply.

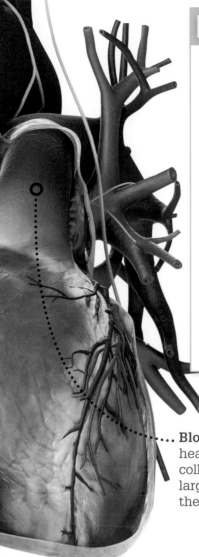

FAST FACTS

The amount of blood pumped by the heart in a minute is known as "cardiac output." This can be used to measure a person's level of fitness. The more blood pumped, the more work their bodies can do.

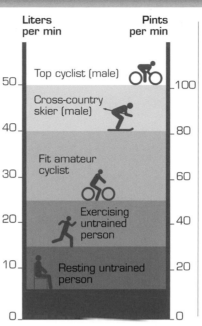

Liters per min		Pints per min
50	Top cyclist (male)	100
40	Cross-country skier (male)	80
30	Fit amateur cyclist	60
20	Exercising untrained person	40
10	Resting untrained person	20
0		0

Women	Men	Pregnant women
8 pints (4.5 liters)	8¾ pints (5 liters)	11½ pints (6.5 liters)

On average, women have slightly less blood than men. An average pregnant woman, however, has more blood than a man. This extra blood is used to carry nutrients and oxygen to her baby.

Blood travels from the heart to the lungs to collect oxygen through a large blood vessel called the pulmonary artery.

An adult heart pumps enough blood to fill 5.3 10,000-gallon (38,000-liter) road tankers every month.

The heart has *a left* and a right side. The right side delivers blood to the lungs to pick up oxygen. The left side pumps this oxygen-rich blood around the body to deliver nutrients to all the body's cells. The cells absorb the oxygen, and the oxygen-poor blood returns to the heart to start its journey again.

The heart pumps oxygen-rich blood to the body through arteries (shown in red). This blood is bright red because it contains hemoglobin, the substance that carries the oxygen. Oxygen-poor blood is dark red.

How **long** are your **blood vessels?**

It is estimated that there may be as many as **100,000 miles** (160,000 km) of blood vessels in an **adult's body,** and **60,000 miles** (97,000 km) in a **child's.**

There are three main types of blood vessel: arteries, veins, and capillaries. They cover such a great distance because they need to reach every cell in your body, delivering oxygen and nutrients and carrying away the cells' waste.

Blood leaves the heart and travels in arteries (shown in red) to the tissues and returns in veins (blue).

In the tissues, arteries (such as the two seen in each finger here) branch out into many smaller blood vessels, called capillaries.

COLD FINGERS

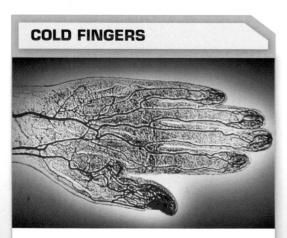

Although arteries (shown in red in this false-color scan) reach to the ends of the fingers, sometimes hands can feel cold. This is because the body may restrict the blood flow to the hands to keep the rest of the body warm.

FAST FACTS

Capillary

Some capillaries are so narrow that only one blood cell at a time can pass through them. The widest blood vessel is an artery called the aorta. At its widest, the aorta is about 1¼ in (3 cm) across—about 6,000 times wider than the narrowest capillary.

Veins
65% of blood volume

Arteries
35% of blood volume

There is more blood in the body's veins than in the arteries at any one time. Veins are wider inside than arteries (because they have thinner walls), and blood moves more slowly through them.

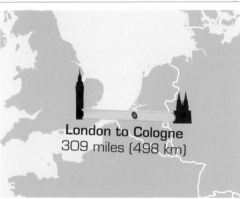

London to Cologne
309 miles (498 km)

A red blood cell is thought to travel 2.5 miles (4 km) around your body every day. Over its lifetime of about 120 days, a cell will cover 300 miles (480 km)—that's just under the distance from London to Cologne, Germany.

An **adult human's** network of **blood vessels** would **circle the world four times**.

Capillaries are thin—about 20 of the narrowest can fit across the width of a hair. These are just wide enough for one red blood cell to travel through at a time. Their thin walls let substances pass between the blood and the body tissues.

How much air do you breathe in a lifetime?

Based on a life span of **70 years**, the average human breathes around 9.7 million cubic feet (275 million liters) of air.

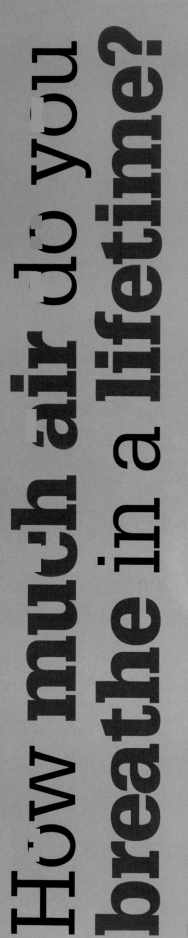

An average-sized hot-air balloon, capable of carrying three to five people, contains 616,000 gallons (2,800,000 liters) of air.

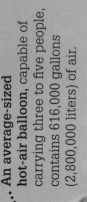

Over a lifetime, the average human breathes enough air to fill around 95–100 hot-air balloons.

FLAT-HEADED FROG

Most frogs breathe through both their lungs and skin, but this rare Bornean flat-headed frog, which grows up to 3 in [7.7 cm] long, has no lungs. It is the only known frog to breathe only through its skin.

The windpipe is the tube in the chest and throat that carries air in and out of the lungs.

An adult's lungs take in an average of about 1 pint (0.5 liters) of air in each breath and breathe about 15 times a minute when sitting down.

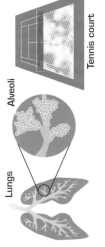

Human lungs

FAST FACTS

Lungs   Alveoli

Tennis court

The average adult's lungs contain 300–500 million tiny round sacs called alveoli—enough to cover about half a tennis court.

Bar-headed goose
21,670 ft (6,300 m)

Himalayan mountain pass
18,000 ft (5,500 m)

Bar-headed geese have very efficient lungs and can cross the Himalayas at altitudes of around 21,670 ft (6,300 m), where there is very little oxygen. Humans cannot live permanently at such extreme heights.

How **heavy** are your **bones?**

Bones are actually very **light**—your **skeleton** accounts for only about **15 percent** of your **total weight.**

INSIDE A BONE

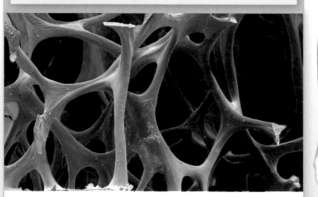

Although very strong, bones are light because they are not solid. Inside the hard, dense "compact bone" is "spongy bone," which looks like honeycomb (shown here in this false-colored image). The spaces in the bone are filled with jellylike marrow.

The hyoid bone in the throat is one of the few bones that isn't joined to another.

An **adult human** weighs more than **six times** the weight of **its skeleton**.

Your feet and hands contain more than half of your body's bones—27 in each foot and 26 in each hand.

FAST FACTS

Babies are born with around 300 bones. As they grow up, many of the bones—such as those in the skull—fuse together, so most adults have 206 bones.

Adult skull   **Baby skull**

3,821 lb (1,733 kg)

Piece of bone

Bone is incredibly strong. A cube of bone measuring ½ in (1 cm) along each side would be able to support 3,821 lb (1,733 kg)—the weight of an adult male hippo.

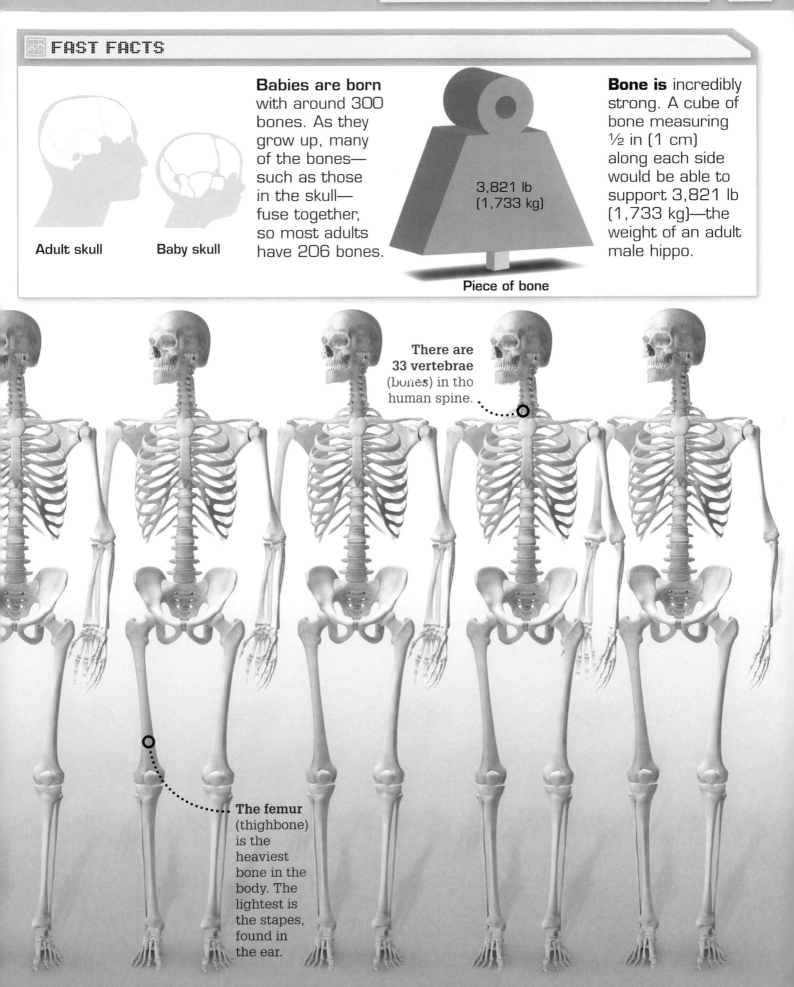

There are 33 vertebrae (bones) in tho human spine.

The femur (thighbone) is the heaviest bone in the body. The lightest is the stapes, found in the ear.

FAST FACTS

Large eyes give animals the brightest, sharpest vision possible. Tarsiers have some of the largest eyes relative to their body size. They need them to hunt for insects in the rain forest at night. Each of their eyes is as big as their brain! A human's eyes are proportionally much smaller.

Tarsier brain and eye
relative sizes

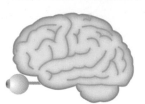

Human brain and eye
relative sizes

What has the biggest eyes?

The **colossal squid**, a little-known species of squid bigger than the giant squid, has **eyes** up to **11 in** (27 cm) across in the few individuals measured.

PREHISTORIC VISION

Extinct reptiles called ichthyosaurs had eyes up to 12 in (30 cm) across. Like huge squid species, some probably hunted in the deep sea, their big eyes helping them to see in the dim light.

Human eyeball (life-size)
1 in (2.5 cm) across

Horse eyeball (life-size)
1½ in (4 cm) across

The lens of the colossal squid's eye is ball-shaped and about the size of an orange.

The largest colossal squid eye ever studied was a dead one that had the same diameter as 11 human eyeballs.

Blue whale eyeball (life-size) 6 in (15 cm) across

Colossal squid eyeball (life-size) 11 in (27 cm) across. (Experts think the colossal squid's eyes may grow to 12–16 in (30–40 cm) across—as big as a beach ball!)

What has the biggest teeth?

African elephants have the **biggest teeth** of all animals. They have **enormous chewing teeth**, which crush vegetation, and two **huge front teeth** called **tusks.**

Up to 10 deep ridges line the top of the African elephant's molar, ideal for grinding tree branches.

The roots sit below the surface of the gum. When the molar first forms, the roots point down, but as the tooth moves forward in the jaw, the roots slant backward.

Around 65 human molars can fit on top of one elephant molar.

VIPERFISH TEETH

A viperfish's teeth are so long they curve around the outside of its head when it closes its mouth. The glassy daggers are perfectly suited for catching fish that live in the darkest depths of the ocean.

Human molars are on average ¾ in (2 cm) from the crown to the root. Humans grow only two sets of teeth in their lifetime.

An elephant has four molars (back teeth) in its jaws at any one time. They grow up to 8¼ in (21 cm) long and 2¾ in (7 cm) wide, and weigh up to 9 lb (4 kg). Although tooth enamel is the hardest substance in a body, the teeth still wear down and are replaced six times during the elephant's life.

The crown is the part of a tooth that sits above the gum.

FAST FACTS

Tusks are front teeth used for defense while fighting, digging, lifting, or displaying. Walruses also use theirs like icepicks to haul themselves out of the water.

African elephant tusk 10 ft (3 m)

Narwhal tusk 9 ft (2.7 m)

Walrus tusk 3 ft 4 in (1 m)

Warthog tusk 18 in (45 cm)

Babirusa tusk 12 in (30 cm)

An ancient sharklike fish called *Helicoprion* had no teeth in its upper jaw and a unique set in its lower jaw—they were arranged like a spiral saw. No one is sure how the fish used them. Perhaps the teeth shredded the flesh of the fish as it pushed it toward its throat to swallow it.

Saw teeth spiraled out of its mouth

The creases in the root show that a molar is made up of a collection of up to 12 separate plates, or "tooth buds," that merged together as they grew.

A lion's back teeth are around 1¼ in (3 cm) wide. They are razor-sharp and work in pairs, like scissors, to slice through meat.

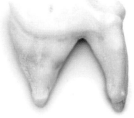

A great white shark has serrated teeth. The largest can grow to 2¾ in (7 cm) from base to tip.

All teeth are shown life-size

Body data

ORGANIZING THE BODY

Cells, the building blocks of the body, organize themselves into more **complex structures** called **tissues**. Tissues, in turn, combine to form **organs**, which make up the **systems** that **control the body's functions.** The body **has many different systems**, including the nervous system (right).

TISSUE

CELL

ORGAN

SYSTEM

VITAL INGREDIENTS

An average adult human contains:

enough **phosphorus** to make **220 matches**

enough **iron** to make a

nail 3 in (7 cm) long

enough **carbon** to fill **900 pencils**

enough **fat** for **75 candles**

KEEPING US **COMPANY**

In an average human body, there are approximately

100 trillion cells.

But each person is also home to around **10 times this number of bacteria.** Gathered together, these bacteria would fill a **½ gallon (2 liter) container**.

BREATHE **DEEPLY**

The rate at which humans breathe depends on what they're doing—ranging from about **12–15 breaths per minute** while **resting** to **45–50 breaths per minute** when **exercising hard**.

IN THEIR LIFETIME, **THE AVERAGE HUMAN WILL:**

- grow **92 ft** (28 m) of fingernails—just a little longer than a standard-sized swimming pool
- spend a total of **3 years** going to the bathroom •
produce **10,500 gallons** (40,000 liters) of urine •
work for **9 years** • shed around **560 lb** (250 kg)
of dead skin • blink **415 million** times • talk for
12 years • grow **590 miles** (950 km) of hair on
their head—that's around the length of the UK.

REPRODUCTION

- Elephants have a long gestation period—they carry a single baby for **22 months** before giving birth.

- Termite queens can lay up to **30,000 eggs** a day.

- The ocean sunfish can produce more eggs than any other known vertebrate. Each breeding season, the fish scatters up to **300 million tiny eggs** into the ocean.

FEEDING TIME

An adult blue whale can eat as much as **3.8 tons (3.5 metric tons)** of krill (tiny crustaceans) per day—about the weight of **3 small cars.**

Adult mayflies eat **nothing at all**. An adult mayfly lives for just a few hours, during which time it spends most of its time breeding.

BIG & SMALL

An adult human body contains

206 bones.

The **longest** is the femur in the upper leg. The shortest are three tiny bones called ossicles in the ear.

EAR OSSICLES (ACTUAL SIZE)

FEMUR (ACTUAL SIZE)

HEARING RANGES

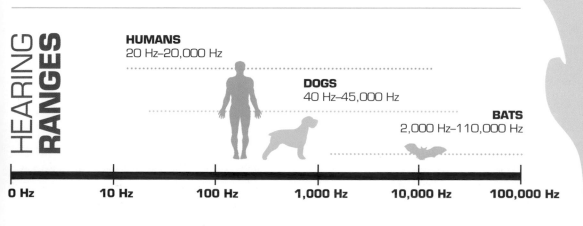

HUMANS
20 Hz–20,000 Hz

DOGS
40 Hz–45,000 Hz

BATS
2,000 Hz–110,000 Hz

| 0 Hz | 10 Hz | 100 Hz | 1,000 Hz | 10,000 Hz | 100,000 Hz |

What is the biggest living thing?

California's giant sequoia trees are the most **massive**, or heaviest, life-forms. They can weigh up to 2,105 tons (1,910 metric tons).

TUNNEL TREES

In the 1800s and early 1900s, people cut tunnels out of giant sequoias to allow carriages or cars to drive through them. These "tunnel trees" were tourist attractions, designed to advertise California's national parks. No new tunnels are cut today, but some old ones still exist.

Giant sequoias would grow even taller, but lightning kills off their upper branches.

Forest ecologist studying the top parts of the tree.

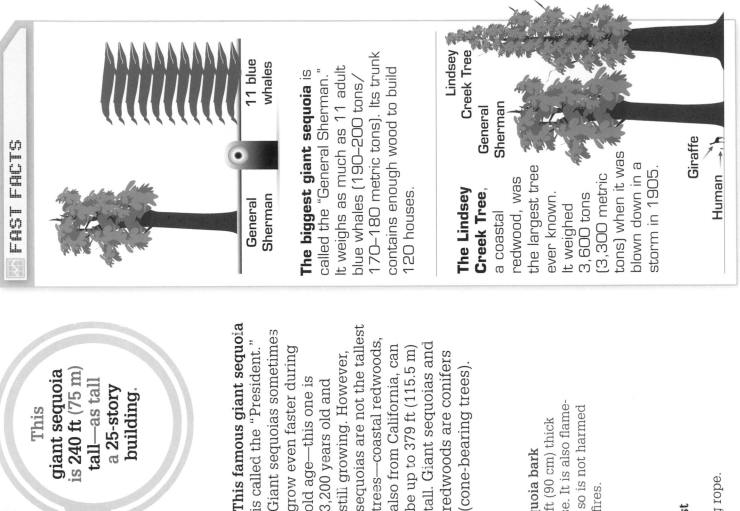

11 blue whales

General Sherman

The biggest giant sequoia is called the "General Sherman." It weighs as much as 11 adult blue whales (190–200 tons/ 170–180 metric tons). Its trunk contains enough wood to build 120 houses.

Lindsey Creek Tree

General Sherman

Giraffe

Human

The Lindsey Creek Tree, a coastal redwood, was the largest tree ever known. It weighed 3,600 tons (3,300 metric tons) when it was blown down in a storm in 1905.

This **giant sequoia is 240 ft (75 m) tall**—as tall a 25-story building.

This famous giant sequoia is called the "President." Giant sequoias sometimes grow even faster during old age—this one is 3,200 years old and still growing. However, sequoias are not the tallest trees—coastal redwoods, also from California, can be up to 379 ft (115.5 m) tall. Giant sequoias and redwoods are conifers (cone-bearing trees).

Forest ecologist climbing tree.

Giant sequoia bark may be 3 ft (90 cm) thick at the base. It is also flame-resistant, so is not harmed by forest fires.

Forest ecologist holding climbing rope.

How big is the biggest animal?

The **largest animal** on the **planet** is the **blue whale**, measuring **100 ft** (30 m). It is the **biggest** animal that has **ever lived**, including the **dinosaurs.**

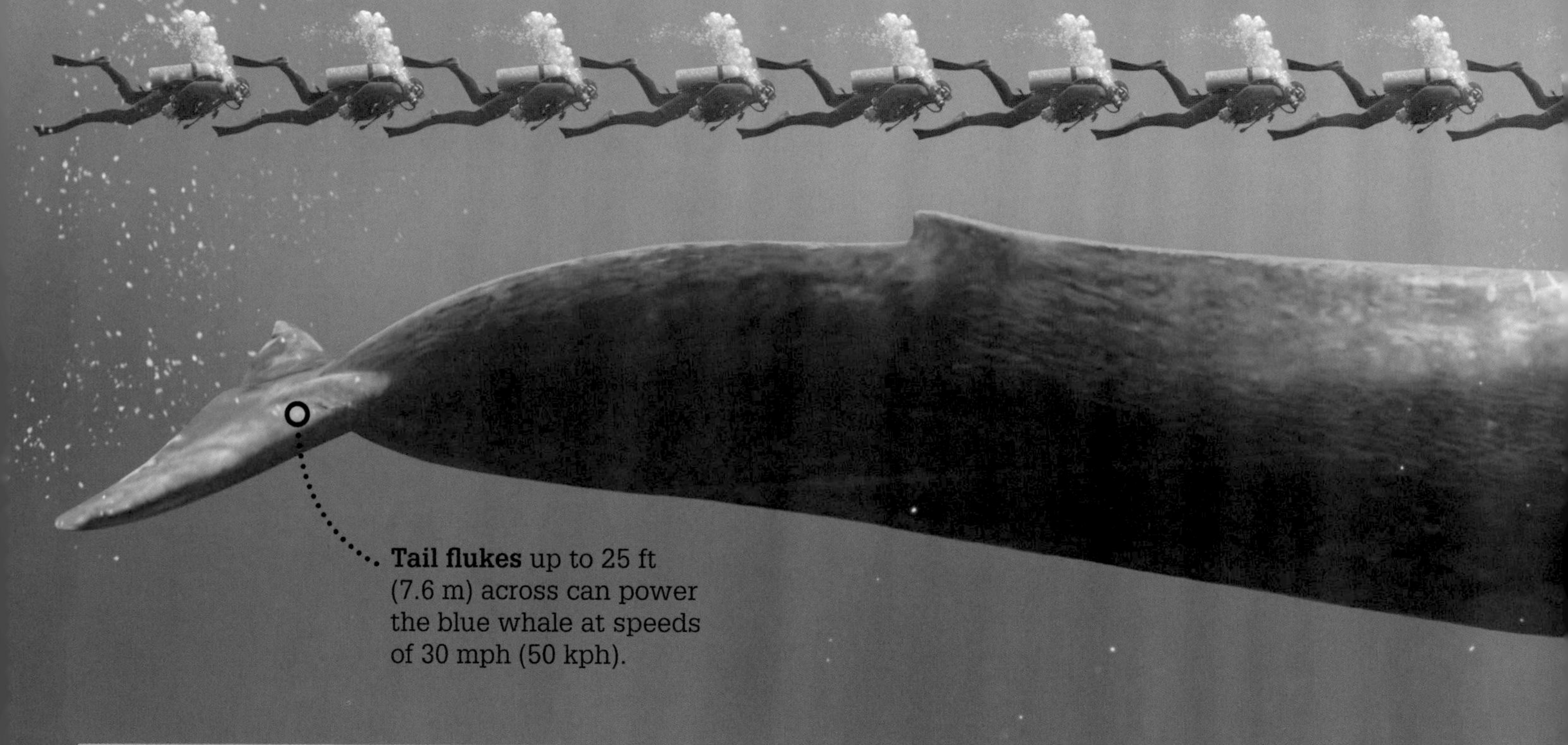

Tail flukes up to 25 ft (7.6 m) across can power the blue whale at speeds of 30 mph (50 kph).

FAST FACTS

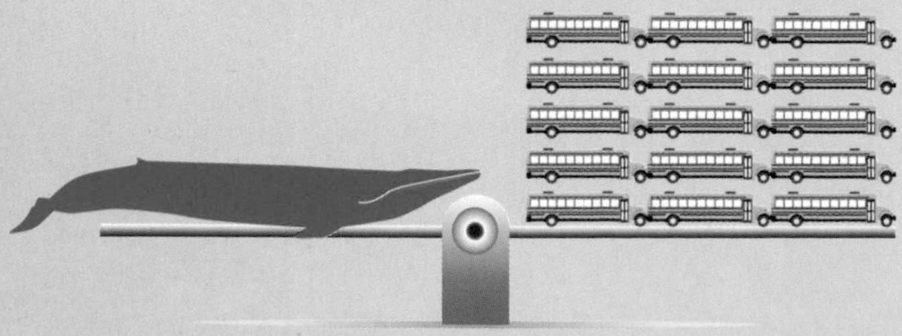

A blue whale is longer than a basketball court and weighs up to 200 tons (180 tonnes)—the same as 15 school buses.

Blue whales make a noise louder than a jet aircraft taking off. Whales produce very low frequency sounds at a level of 188 decibels; these can be heard from thousands of miles away.

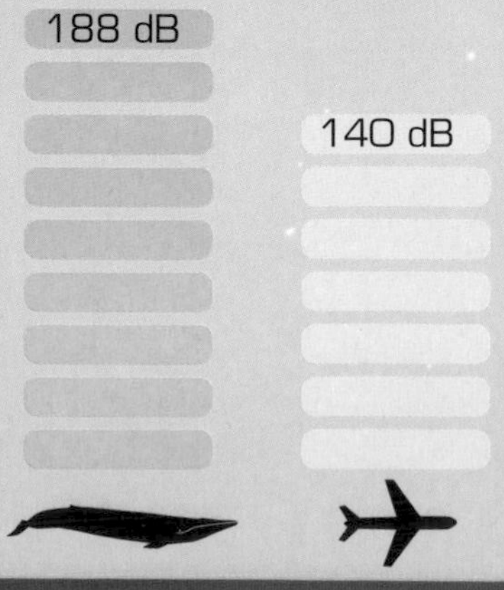

188 dB

140 dB

FILTER FEEDING

A blue whale can eat around 4 tons (3.5 metric tons) of krill (tiny sea creatures) a day. Taking 100-ton (90-metric-ton) gulps of water, the whale then filters the water out through baleen plates, comblike structures that hang from its jaw, trapping the krill.

The blue whale's heart is the size of a small car.

Its eyeball is 6 in (15 cm) in diameter.

Its tongue weighs as much as an elephant.

Its outer ear is the width of a pencil tip.

A blue whale is as long as 17 scuba divers swimming in a line.

A blue whale can blow 160 cu ft (4,500 liters) of air out of its blowholes at 300 mph (480 kph). The spray it produces reaches a height of 30 ft (9 m)—as tall as five men standing on each others' heads.

Argentinosaurus started life as an egg the size of a soccer ball. Once hatched, the baby dinosaur weighed around 11 lb (5 kg). It took nearly 40 years to reach its adult weight. No one knows why it grew so big, but its long neck would have helped it to reach the leaves of the tall trees that it ate.

BEFORE THE DINOSAURS

Long before the dinosaurs, there were no large animals on land—but there were in the oceans. *Pterygotus*, a giant sea scorpion that lived 400 million years ago, grew to 7 ft 6 in (2.3 m) long—bigger than an adult human.

The long neck weighed about 6½ tons (6 metric tons), even though the neck bones were hollow and filled with air, making them lighter than normal bone.

Argentinosaurus had a small head because it didn't need heavy jaws to chew its food— it simply gulped it down.

This **dinosaur** stood as tall as a **double-decker bus** at the shoulder and **weighed** the same as 25 elephants.

Double-decker bus
14 ft 6 in (4.4 m) tall

Adult man
5 ft 11 in (1.8 m) tall

Argentinosaurus
115 ft (35 m) long

What was the biggest dinosaur?

Argentinosaurus is the **longest, heaviest** dinosaur whose size we can accurately judge. It weighed up to **83 tons** (75 metric tons). As **fossil hunters** unearth **more bones**, they may prove that **even bigger dinosaurs** existed.

The dinosaur's tail may have been used for support as it reared up on its hind legs to reach high tree branches.

📊 FAST FACTS

Argentinosaurus was the biggest of a family called the sauropods. Even one of the smallest, *Europasaurus*, was 20 ft (6 m) long and weighed up to 1.1 ton (1 metric tons).

Europasaurus   *Argentinosaurus*

Human

Pliosaur

Among the biggest prehistoric beasts living in the sea were pliosaurs. The largest of these were over 50 ft (15 m) long.

What was the biggest land predator?

The **biggest predator** that ever lived **on land** was *Spinosaurus*, a **56-ft-** (17-m-) long fish-eating **dinosaur**.

Spinosaurus was the longest predatory dinosaur known. It lived around 100 million years ago in North Africa.

This adult man stands about 5 ft 11 in (1.8 m) tall.

A male polar bear is the biggest land predator today. It can grow up to 10 ft (3 m) in length and be 5 ft (1.5 m) tall at the shoulder.

Spinosaurus's size was enhanced by long spines extending up from its backbone, which probably created a tall crest or "sail."

Spinosaurus was more than five times the length of a polar bear.

The dinosaur's huge tail balanced the weight of its head and forelimbs, allowing it to walk on its hind legs.

SABER-TOOTHED CAT

Smilodon was the biggest cat to walk the Earth. At 6 ft 6 in (2 m) long, it was big enough to attack and eat mammoths. The cat probably wrestled its prey to the ground, then killed it with its large canine teeth.

FAST FACTS

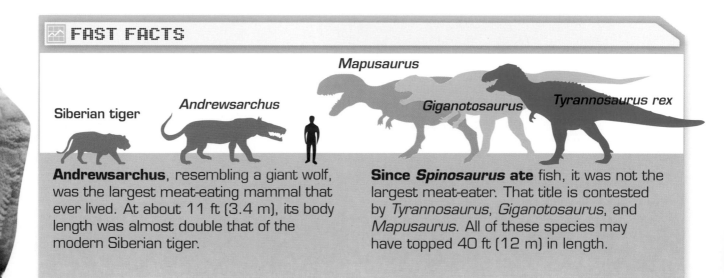

Siberian tiger

Andrewsarchus

Mapusaurus

Giganotosaurus

Tyrannosaurus rex

Andrewsarchus, resembling a giant wolf, was the largest meat-eating mammal that ever lived. At about 11 ft (3.4 m), its body length was almost double that of the modern Siberian tiger.

Since Spinosaurus ate fish, it was not the largest meat-eater. That title is contested by *Tyrannosaurus*, *Giganotosaurus*, and *Mapusaurus*. All of these species may have topped 40 ft (12 m) in length.

What was the largest snake?

Titanoboa was an **enormous snake** measuring **48 ft** (14.6 m), or longer than a school bus. It lived around **60 million years ago** in the **jungle swamps** of modern-day **Colombia**.

EATING HABITS

Big snakes such as pythons can eat prey wider than themselves. The snake cannot chew, so prey must be swallowed whole. Digesting food uses so much energy, the snake is inactive for several days.

Like the jaws of today's snakes, the lower jaw would unhinge, enabling *Titanoboa* to swallow large prey.

Snakes breathe through a hole called the glottis. This can move to the side so that the reptile can breathe as it slowly swallows its prey.

Titanoboa's coloring is unknown. The pattern on this illustration is based on the anaconda, one of the biggest snakes alive today.

The middle of the trunk was much widor than the ends of the snake. At its widest, it was 3 ft (90 cm) in diameter.

The **thickest** part of *Titanoboa*'s body was **half the height of a man**.

Titanoboa **weighed** more than 1 tonne (1 ton)—as much as a small family car and big enough to tackle giant turtles and crocodiles. Experts have argued that it grew so big because the world was warmer 60 million years ago, and reptiles today are usually bigger in warmer climates.

📊 FAST FACTS

The longest snakes alive today are little more than half the length of *Titanoboa*.

King cobra 18 ft (5.5 m)

Indian python 21 ft (6.4 m)

Green anaconda 29 ft (9 m)

Reticulated python 33 ft (10 m)

Megalodon's tail fin provided all the propulsion the shark needed while swimming and hunting.

How **big** was the **biggest shark?**

MOSASAUR

Megalodon was one of the world's biggest-ever hunters, but many other ocean predators have grown to monstrous lengths. The 49-ft (15-m) *Mosasaurus* lived around 65 million years ago.

The **largest shark** that ever lived was **megalodon**, which may have grown to **66 ft** (20 m) **long.** It died out more than **1.5 million years ago.**

Megalodon's dorsal fin may have been taller than a man.

The pectoral fin provided lift, stopping the shark from sinking.

Some experts think megalodon was very similar to today's great white shark, but much bigger. It may not have been closely related, however. It lived in all the world's oceans and first appeared around 17–16 million years ago.

Megalodon may have grown to be between 7 and 11 times the length of an adult scuba diver.

FAST FACTS

Today's biggest shark is not the great white, but the whale shark, a gentle giant that feeds on plankton—tiny floating creatures. The great white is the biggest predatory shark—one that hunts down individual prey, such as fish.

Megalodon's huge teeth are the most common fossil remains of the creature. They are the same shape as the teeth of the great white shark, but more than three times the height.

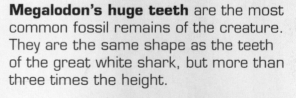

Megalodon
52–65 ft
(16–20 m) long,
55 tons (50 metric tons)

Whale shark
41ft 6 in (12.65 m)
long, 23.5 tons
(21.5 metric tons)

Great white shark
20 ft (6.1 m) long,
2 tons (1.9 metric tons)

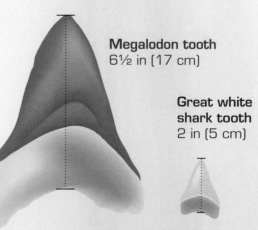

Megalodon tooth
6½ in (17 cm)

Great white shark tooth
2 in (5 cm)

The spider's leg span is measured from the tip of one leg to the tip of the opposite leg.

The spider's fangs, which are 1 in (2.5 cm) long, are tucked under the hair-covered upper mouthparts.

The hairs covering the spider's body can cause rashes and swelling on human skin. The tarantula flicks them at attackers to defend itself.

The Goliath bird-eater is a species of tarantula and lives in South America. It grows big enough to eat birds, although it mostly eats insects, rodents, bats, snakes, and lizards. It pounces on prey and injects it with venom from its fangs.

Goliaths can grow to be bigger than an adult's hand and can cover a dinner plate!

GIANT HUNTSMAN SPIDER

The longest spider legs are thought to belong to the giant huntsman spider of Laos, Southeast Asia. Its legs span up to 12 in (30 cm), although its body is just 1¾ in (4.6 cm) long.

How big can spiders grow?

The Goliath bird-eater rubs bristles on its legs to produce a hissing sound as a warning to predators.

The **heaviest type** of spider is the **goliath bird-eating spider**, which can **weigh** up to **6 oz** (175 g). The biggest one measured had a **leg span** of **11 in** (28 cm).

📈 FAST FACTS

Darwin's bark spiders can spin webs up to 80 ft (25 m)—as wide a six-lane highway. Its silk is highly resistant to breaking and more than 10 times tougher than Kevlar (a material used to make body armor).

Most spiders are venomous, and some species have venom deadly enough to kill dozens of mice. Most spiders are harmless to humans, but these three demand respect.

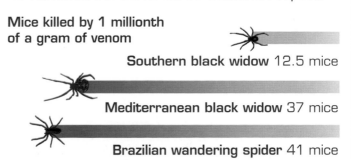

Mice killed by 1 millionth of a gram of venom

Southern black widow 12.5 mice

Mediterranean black widow 37 mice

Brazilian wandering spider 41 mice

What is the biggest insect?

There are several contenders, but the **Atlas moth** has the biggest wings, with a **span** of **10 in** (25 cm) and a **wing area** of **62 sq in** (400 sq cm).

The Atlas moth is much **bigger** than an adult **human hand**.

GIANT WETA

The giant weta, one of the world's heaviest insects, lives in New Zealand. Wetas gnaw roots and stems in their forest habitat and have grown to mouselike sizes. At 2½ oz (70 g), the largest are as big as three house mice.

The fat abdomen of the female contains an egg factory.

The Atlas moth of Southeast Asia is the biggest insect by wing area. However, the white witch moth of Central and South America has the widest wingspan, at about 12 in (31 cm).

These narrow antennae tell us this is a female, which is even larger and heavier than a male. The male has bigger, more feathery antennae, and he uses them to detect pheromones (scent) released by females.

The wing tip looks like a snake's head, which possibly frightens would-be predators.

The triangular patterns on the moth's wings are thought to help camouflage.

FAST FACTS

There are other insects competing for the title of the biggest insect alive. Here are some of the contenders.

Rat

Titan beetle

The titan beetle of South American rain forests grows up to 6.5 in (16.5 cm) long—as long as than the body of a rat. Its jaws can snap a pencil in half.

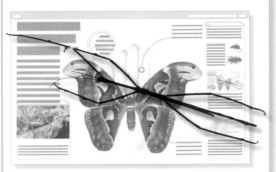

Stick insects can be even longer. The record-breaking Chan's megastick of Borneo, Malaysia, is 22½ in (56.7 cm) long with outstretched legs. That's longer than this book.

Goliath beetle grub

Some insects have really large grubs. One of the biggest and heaviest is that of Africa's Goliath beetle. It can grow up to 5 in (13 cm) long and weighs 3½ oz (100 g).

Running along the front edge of *Quetzalcoatlus*'s wing were the incredibly long bones of a single finger, which held the wing open.

The **wings** of *Quetzalcoatlus* stretched farther than those of a Tiger Moth biplane.

What had the longest wings ever?

The **largest flying creature** was a **pterosaur** called *Quetzalcoatlus*. It soared over its relatives, the **dinosaurs**, 68 million years ago. The largest had a **wingspan** of **more than 33 ft** (10 m).

📊 FAST FACTS

Here's how Quetzalcoatlus's wingspan compares to some other giant flyers.

Argentavis lived 6 million years ago and—with a wingspan of 23 ft (7 m)—was the largest flying bird ever.

The great bustard is today's heaviest flying bird and has a wingspan of 8 ft 3 in (2.5 m).

Quetzalcoatlus lived 68–66 million years ago and measured 33 ft (10 m) from wing tip to wing tip.

The wandering albatross has the longest wings of any living bird, at 11 ft 6 in (3.5 m).

Quetzalcoatlus was very thin and light in the central body and neck, so, despite its colossal dimensions, even this 33-ft (10-m) individual probably weighed less than 550 lb (250 kg). This is still twice as heavy as an ostrich.

A Tiger Moth has a wingspan of 29 ft (8.9 m). Originally designed to train military pilots in the 1930s, it can carry two people. It is still famous and popular with pilots today.

MONSTER BIRDS

Teratornis (left) was an ancient bird that was similar to a modern condor, but bigger and heavier. Its close relative, *Argentavis*, was gigantic and weighed as much as a person.

At only 2½ in (5.5 cm) long, the bee hummingbird can perch on the end of a pencil.

The male bee hummingbird has a glossy pink head and throat and is even smaller than the female.

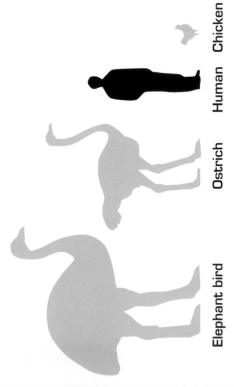

FAST FACTS

Actual size

The bee hummingbird builds a cup-shaped nest about 1 in (2.5 cm) across from bits of cobwebs, bark, and lichen. Nests have been built on single clothes pins. The eggs are the size of peas.

In contrast, the heaviest living bird that can fly is the great bustard. At 46 lb (20.9 kg), it weighs as much as a six-year-old boy.

Great Bustard

Elephant bird   Ostrich   Human   Chicken

Today's heaviest bird, the ostrich, can weigh nearly twice as much as an adult person. However, a few hundred years ago, an even heavier bird—the elephant bird—lived in Madagascar. It weighed as much as three ostriches. It is now extinct.

What is the smallest bird?

The bee hummingbird, which lives only in Cuba, is 2¼ in (5.5 cm) long and **weighs** just 0.06 oz (1.6 g).

The bee hummingbird is a tiny but busy bird. It hovers by flapping its wings at 80 times a second, with its heart beating at an incredible 1,220 times a minute. To power this activity, the bird must feed every 10–15 minutes. It eats about half its own body weight in sugary nectar every day.

THE SWORD-BILLED HUMMINGBIRD

Not all hummingbirds are tiny. Among the largest are sword-billed hummingbirds. Their bills alone measure the same as two entire bee hummingbirds!

Which bird laid the biggest egg?

Eggs of the extinct **elephant bird** were up to **13 in (34 cm) long.** Elephant birds lived in **Madagascar** until a few hundred years ago.

Emu

Emu eggs are unusually dark. They look like a huge avocado, at 5 in (13 cm) high.

A kiwi is 20 times smaller than an emu, but its eggs are almost the same size.

Hummingbird eggs are the smallest bird eggs. This one is from a ruby-throated hummingbird.

Rusty tinamou

Hummingbird

Chicken

The most familiar eggs are laid by the domestic chicken.

King penguin

Quail

Kiwi

Common sandpiper

Cormorant

Tawny owl

📈 FAST FACTS

Elephant bird eggs are bigger than those of most dinosaurs. Even the eggs of sauropods (the biggest dinosaurs) are no more than 8 in (20 cm) long. Recent digs in China, however, appear to have turned up giant eggs of two-legged dinosaurs similar to *Oviraptor*.

24 in (60 cm)

13 in (33 cm)

8 in (20 cm)

| Elephant bird 10 ft (3 m) tall | Sauropod up to 120 ft (36 m) long | Giant *Oviraptor* 26 ft (8 m) long |

Elephant birds had died out by the 18th century, but a few of their eggshells still exist. Most shell remains, however, are found as fragments. Pieces found near the sites of ancient cooking fires suggest that people ate the eggs.

In terms of volume, an elephant bird's egg is as big as **200 chicken eggs** or 11 ostrich eggs.

The shell of the egg is ¼ in (3.8 mm) thick and could bear the weight of about 90 bricks (550 lb/248 kg).

Ostrich

The ostrich is the world's largest bird, and it lays the biggest eggs today—although they are the smallest in relation to the size of the mother. They weigh on average just over 3 lb (1.4 kg)—more than 20 chicken eggs.

Elephant bird

Cetti's warbler

Guillemot

Guillemot eggs roll in circles, so they don't fall off cliff ledges, where they are laid.

Great auk

Carrion crow

Curlew

KIWI EGGS

Kiwis lay the biggest eggs in relation to their body size. One egg can be up to one-fifth of the weight of its mother.

Sparrowhawk

Cuckoo

Redshank

How far can a bird fly?

Bar-tailed godwits have been tracked flying **7,258 miles** (11,680 km) **nonstop** from Alaska to New Zealand on their **yearly migration.**

China
North Korea
South Korea
Japan
Philippines
Indonesia
Papua New Guinea
Australia

FAST FACTS

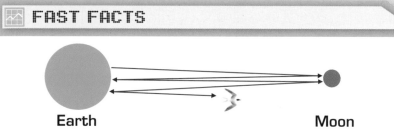

Earth   Moon

Arctic terns migrate from the Arctic to the Antarctic and back every year. Single birds have been tracked flying 44,000 miles (70,900 km) in this time. In their 30-year lifetime, they can cover 1.3 million miles (2.1 million km), or more than two round trips to the Moon.

Glider 1,870 miles (3,009 km)

Airliner (Boeing 777 specially adapted for record attempt) 13,423 miles (21,602 km)

Breitling Orbiter balloon 25,361 miles (40,814 km)

Virgin Atlantic GlobalFlyer 25,766 miles (41,467 km)

An airliner can fly farther than any bird if it is specially adapted. Above are four human nonstop flight records involving different kinds of aircraft.

Every year in March, Pacific bar-tailed godwits fly north from New Zealand. They arrive in Alaska to nest in May, after refueling in China. Scientists know the return journey to New Zealand can be direct and nonstop.

Russia

Alaska

Breeding grounds in the Yukon Delta of Alaska become a godwit's home in the summer, when the bird brings up its chicks.

A **bar-tailed godwit** can, without landing, **fly farther than most airliners.**

The Airbus 320 is a short-to-medium-range [air]ner. Flying from Alaska, it [w]ould run out of fuel long [befo]re the godwit, and would [ha]ve to land at Wake Island in the Pacific.

The godwit's curved route goes over Hawaii, extending the journey.

3,527 miles (5,676 km)

Pacific Ocean

6,583 miles (10,595 km)

7,261 miles (11,686 km)

The Boeing 777-300 is [a] long-range airliner, but with 368 passengers on board, it [w]ould not reach New Zealand. It would have to land at [N]orfolk Island, between New Zealand and Australia.

LIFE ON THE WING

Most swifts rarely land between leaving their nest for the first time and building their own nest 2–4 years later. They mate, eat, and sleep in flight. It is not known how much ground they cover in that time.

New Zealand

After spending 8 days in the air, and with the fat in its 1-lb (450-g) body almost used up, the godwit arrives in its wintering grounds in a river estuary in New Zealand.

How **old** is the **oldest tree?**

The world's **oldest living tree** started life in around 3050 BCE, making it more than **5,060 years old**. The tree is a **Great Basin bristlecone pine** in the White Mountains of California.

1804 First steam locomotive is built

c.700 CE Vikings raid northwest Europe

OLDEST SEED

While excavating King Herod's Palace at Masada, Israel, in the 1960s, archeologists found Judean date palm seeds that were at least 2,000 years old. In 2005, one seed successfully sprouted and was planted at Kibbutz Ketura. The tree has been nicknamed "Methuselah," after the Biblical man said to be the oldest person ever to live.

The **oldest bristlecone pine** has lived through all of **recorded human history**.

432 BCE Parthenon is built in Greece

When the world's oldest tree sprouted from its seed, people wrote with pictures and symbols, not letters and words; the wheel was unknown in most of the world; and the great civilization of ancient Egypt was only just beginning.

c.3050 BCE The tree's seed sprouts

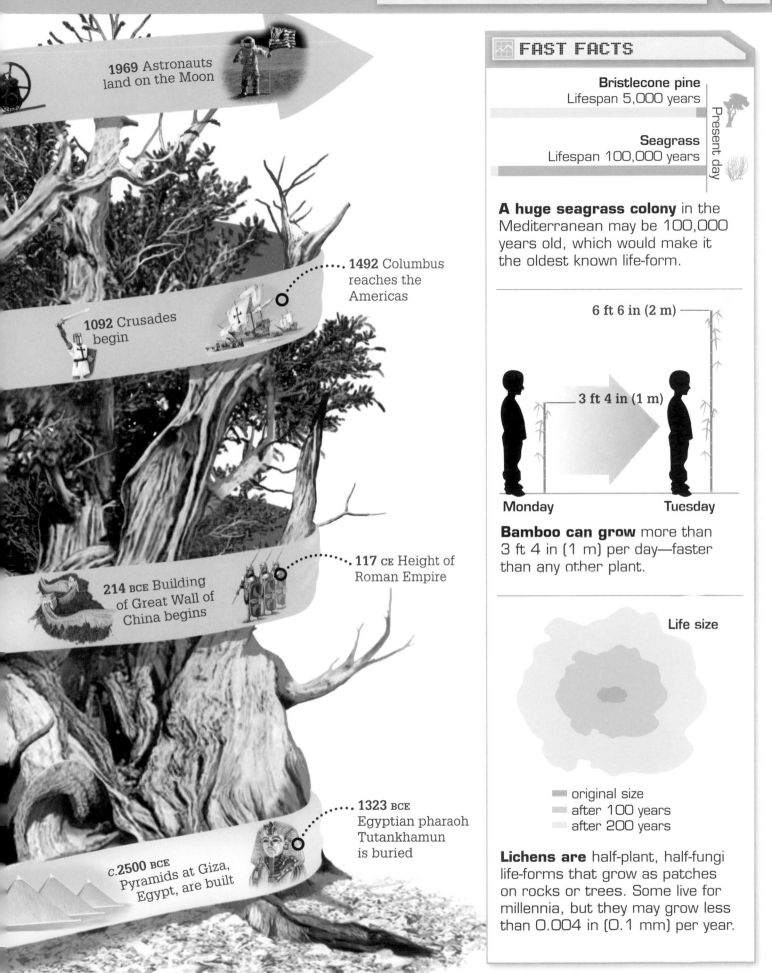

1969 Astronauts land on the Moon

1492 Columbus reaches the Americas

1092 Crusades begin

214 BCE Building of Great Wall of China begins

117 CE Height of Roman Empire

1323 BCE Egyptian pharaoh Tutankhamun is buried

c.2500 BCE Pyramids at Giza, Egypt, are built

FAST FACTS

Bristlecone pine
Lifespan 5,000 years

Seagrass
Lifespan 100,000 years

Present day

A huge seagrass colony in the Mediterranean may be 100,000 years old, which would make it the oldest known life-form.

6 ft 6 in (2 m)

3 ft 4 in (1 m)

Monday — Tuesday

Bamboo can grow more than 3 ft 4 in (1 m) per day—faster than any other plant.

Life size

- original size
- after 100 years
- after 200 years

Lichens are half-plant, half-fungi life-forms that grow as patches on rocks or trees. Some live for millennia, but they may grow less than 0.004 in (0.1 mm) per year.

How **old** are the oldest animals?

Ocean quahog clams are known to live for more than **400 years.** Scientists think some **sponges** may live **even longer.**

ANCIENT SPONGES

It is difficult to identify the age of a sponge, but Caribbean giant barrel sponges (left) have very long lives; one is believed to be 2,300 years old. Some Antarctic glass sponges may live for more than 10,000 years.

Ocean quahogs can live about **5 times** longer than **Asian elephants.**

Human
122 years

Rougheye rockfish
140 years

Most humans don't live 122 years, but there is a verified case of a woman who did.

Asian elephant
86 years

Olm
(a cave salamander)
100 years

Tuatara
111 years

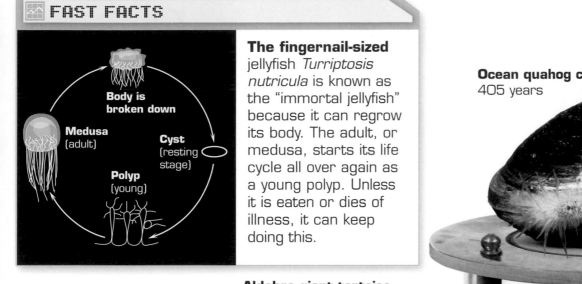

FAST FACTS

Body is
broken down

Medusa
(adult)

Cyst
(resting
stage)

Polyp
(young)

The fingernail-sized jellyfish *Turriptosis nutricula* is known as the "immortal jellyfish" because it can regrow its body. The adult, or medusa, starts its life cycle all over again as a young polyp. Unless it is eaten or dies of illness, it can keep doing this.

The number of growth rings on the shell shows how old the clam is.

Ocean quahog clam
405 years

Aldabra giant tortoise
255 years

The oldest known Aldabra giant tortoise's age was worked out by carbon-dating the shell.

Bowhead whale
211 years

Life-form data

LIFE ON EARTH

Mammals, birds, reptiles, amphibians, and fish are all **vertebrates** (animals with a backbone). Together they make up just **3 percent** of all animal species. **Invertebrates** (animals without a backbone) make up the remaining **97 percent**.

···· VERTEBRATES **3%**

···· INVERTEBRATES **97%**

Nearly one quarter of all the animal species named so far are **beetles**, amounting to around **400,000 species**. In contrast, fewer than 6,000 mammal species have been identified.

THE BIG ONES

The biggest land animals tower over the average human being.

MAN **6 FT** (1.8 M)

BIGGEST BIRD OSTRICH **9 FT** (2.75 M)

BIGGEST LAND ANIMAL ELEPHANT **13 F** (4 M)

TALLEST LAND ANIMAL GIRAFFE **20 FT** (6 M)

BIRDS IN FLIGHT

A bird's **wing-shape** depends on the **way it flies**. Birds that live in open areas have **long wings** suited to **gliding** and **soaring**. Birds that live in dense vegetation have **shorter wings** for flying in **quick bursts**.

SPEED FLYING
Short, light wings for rapid flapping

GLIDING
Long wings for catching sea winds

QUICK TAKEOFF
Powerful wings

SAFETY IN NUMBERS

In 1889, a swarm of locusts with an area of **2,000 sq miles** (5,000 sq km) crossed the Red Sea in the Middle East. It is estimated to have weighed around **500,000 tons** (450,000 metric tons) and contained **250 billion locusts**.

The **African red-billed quelea** is the **most numerous** wild bird species on the planet and forms gigantic flocks.

There are 1.5 billion breeding pairs.

Termite colonies can contain up to

3 million

individuals. The **largest termite mound** ever discovered was

42 ft

(12.8 m) tall.

Argentine ants live in giant groups known as **mega-colonies**. One of the **largest** is believed to stretch for

3,700 miles (6,000 km)

along Europe's Mediterranean coast.

MICRO WORLD

A single gram of soil can contain **40 million bacteria**.

RAPID MANEUVERS
Short, curved wings for quick direction changes

SOARING
Broad wings for rising gently on thermals

TREES AND PLANTS

The **tallest trees** in the world are the **coast redwoods** of California. The tallest recorded specimen, named Hyperion, stands more than **380 ft** (115 m) high—the height of almost two and a half Statues of Liberty.

COAST REDWOOD **HYPERION 380 FT** (115 M)

Some species of kelp can grow up to **12 in** (30 cm) in a single day.

The rare Southeast Asian plant *Rafflesia arnoldii* (also known as the corpse flower) has the world's

largest, and possibly smelliest, flower.
It measures around **39 in** (1 m) across and stinks of rotting flesh.

The smallest flowering plant is *Wolffia globosa*. It measures just **0.02 in** (0.6 mm) long and **0.01 in** (0.3 mm) wide.

WOLFFIA (ACTUAL SIZE)

GIANT KELP

What is the fastest runner?

The **cheetah** is the **fastest land animal**, but only over short distances. **Horses** are **slower**, but can run **much farther** before they get tired.

The fastest sprinters, running the 100 m in less than 10 seconds, reach their top speed usually during the 60–80 m stretch. If they could sustain this top speed throughout the race, they would run it in 8.4 seconds.

27 mph
(43 kph)

WALKING ON WATER

Basilisk lizards can escape from predators by running across the surface of ponds and rivers. Running at a speed of around 4 mph (6 kph), they can cover a distance of 65 ft (20 m) before they start to sink.

At its **top speed**, a **cheetah** would finish a **100 m sprint** in around **3 seconds**.

A thoroughbred racehorse can gallop at up to 43 mph (70 kph) in races of 2 furlongs (0.25 miles/ 0.4 km). Running at this speed, the horse could complete the 100 m sprint in 5.15 seconds.

43 mph
(70 kph)

FAST FACTS

The cheetah's speed comes from its flexible spine. The cat hunches its spine at the start of a stride, bringing its back feet in front of the forefeet. As the back feet hit the ground and push off, its spine extends, giving the cheetah an extra-long stride.

Snail 0.03 (0.05)
Mouse 8 (13)
Squirrel 13 (21)
Elephant 25 (40)
Human 27 (43)
Domestic cat 30 (48)
Greyhound 43 (70)
African lion 55 (89)
Pronghorn 62 (100)

Top speed in mph (kph)

The garden snail certainly takes its time to move around. However, the domestic cat is quite fast—it could beat an Olympic sprinter if it had to make a run for it.

70 mph
(115 kph)

A cheetah can sprint at incredible speeds to catch its prey, but the chase will only last for about 30–60 seconds, after which the cat gets too tired.

What animal can **jump** the farthest?

GLIDING MAMMALS

Some animals do not jump, but can glide for long distances. For example, the sugar glider of Australia, uses flaps of skin between its limbs to help it glide from tree to tree for up to 165 ft (50 m).

The **snow leopard** of central Asia can **leap** the **farthest** in the animal kingdom. It can cover more than **50 ft** (15 m) in a **single jump**.

30 ft (9 m)

29 ft 4½ in (8.95 m)

15 ft (4.5 m)

The jerboa's long back legs help it to jump 45 times its body length.

FAST FACTS

The common flea is the most impressive jumping creature on the planet for its size. Although it is only 0.06 in (1.5 mm) long, it can leap a distance of 13 in (33 cm)—220 times its body length. Fleas are parasites and spring onto mammals, sometimes including humans, to feed on their blood.

On a human scale, if a 5-ft 11-in (1.8-m) man could jump as far as a flea, he would be able to clear more than three soccer fields laid end to end.

The **snow leopard could easily clear seven large family cars in one leap**.

When it jumps, the red kangaroo can reach a speed of more than 35 mph (56 kph).

The human world record for men's long jump was set by US athlete Mike Powell in 1991.

50 ft (15 m)

Snow leopards live in mountain habitats, where they leap to catch their prey of wild sheep and goats.

What is the fastest flyer?

In level flight, a **white-throated needletail** is the **fastest** bird in the air. It has a **top speed** of **105 mph** (170 kph).

The white-throated needletail is a species of swift. These birds spend most of their time high in the sky hunting for insects, and they rarely land. Needletails travel long distances, breeding in Siberia, China, and Japan, then migrating south to countries such as Australia.

DIVING SPEEDS

The peregrine falcon has the fastest dive of any bird. It flies up high, looking for prey. When it spots a duck or a pigeon, it folds its wings and drops into a steep dive at speeds some estimate at more than 185 mph (300 kph). At the last minute, it stretches out its talons to snatch its victim.

FAST FACTS

Although they walk with a slow waddle, ducks and waders are the fastest flying birds, other than swifts, that have been measured accurately. The great snipe has the fastest recorded migration.

Common swift
69 mph (111 kph)

Great snipe (a wader)
60 mph (97 kph)

Eider duck
47 mph (76 kph)

Birds are the fastest fliers, but among other animals, free-tailed bats are the quickest. Dragonflies are among the speediest insects.

Mexican free-tailed bat
40 mph (64 kph)

Flying fish
37 mph (60 kph)

Dragonfly
30 mph (50 kph)

A white-throated needletail flies fast enough to keep up with a high-speed train.

Long, curved wings slip easily through the air.

This high-speed train has a maximum speed of 125 mph (200 kph), but on a scheduled passenger trip, it averages about 106 mph (171 kph), including stops.

What is the fastest swimmer?

The **speediest swimmer**, the **sailfish**, could travel the length of an Olympic **swimming pool** in **1.6 seconds**—around **13 times faster** than the **human** record holder.

FAST FACTS

Sailfish
68 mph (110 kph)

Striped marlin
50 mph (80 kph)

Blue-fin tuna
44 mph (71 kph)

Blue shark
43 mph (69 kph)

Swordfish
40 mph (64 kph)

Dall's porpoise
35 mph (56 kph)

California sea lion
25 mph (40 kph)

Octopus
25 mph (40 kph)

Gentoo penguin
22 mph (36 kph)

Leatherback turtle
21.5 mph (35 kph)

The fastest swimmers are all fish. At the top is the sailfish, which is an amazing 18.5 mph (30 kph) quicker than its nearest rival, the striped marlin.

Some other sea animals swim fast. However, all are slower than the top five fastest fish, which have perfectly streamlined bodies with powerful muscles built for speed.

5.3 mph (8.6 kph)

An Olympic swimmer can keep up his top sprint speed for only one length of the pool (164 ft/50 m).

67 mph (108 kph)

The fastest personal watercraft can zoom across the water at about 12.5 times the speed of the Olympic swimmer.

68 mph (110 kph)

A sailfish is a predator of the open ocean. It uses its speed and large dorsal fin to herd a shoal of fish into a ball. It then slashes its prey with its long bill.

LONG-DISTANCE SWIMMERS

Polar bears can swim very long distances. Scientists tracked one bear over a 420-mile (675-km) journey. It took nearly 10 days, and the bear didn't stop to eat or sleep.

A sailfish speeds through water at 68 mph (110 kph), faster than a personal watercraft.

How deep can animals go?

Some animals, such as **sea urchins**, can live at a depth of **7 miles** (11 km), at the bottom of **ocean trenches**. Even **air-breathing** animals, which must hold their breath, can **dive** to **7,835 ft** (2,388 m).

LIVING LIGHTS

The deep-sea anglerfish has a fleshy rod growing from its head with a light on the end. In the complete darkness of the deep ocean, this glowing bait lures small fish and shrimp into the predator's gaping jaws.

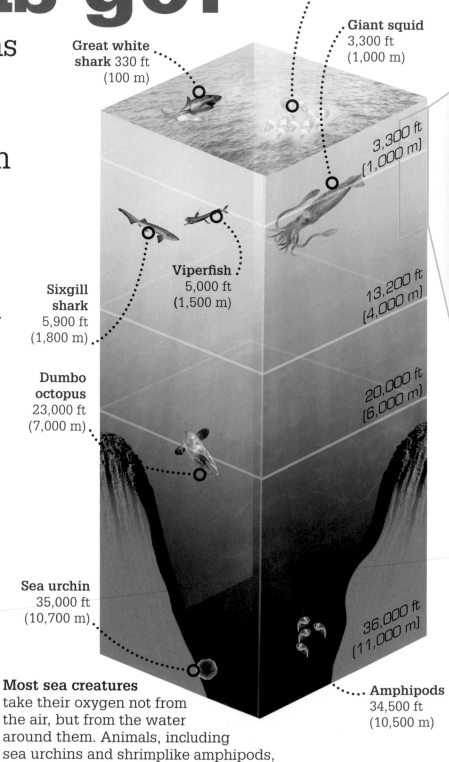

Box jellyfish 12 in (30 cm) deep

Giant squid 3,300 ft (1,000 m)

Great white shark 330 ft (100 m)

3,300 ft (1,000 m)

Viperfish 5,000 ft (1,500 m)

Sixgill shark 5,900 ft (1,800 m)

13,200 ft (4,000 m)

Dumbo octopus 23,000 ft (7,000 m)

20,000 ft (6,000 m)

Sea urchin 35,000 ft (10,700 m)

36,000 ft (11,000 m)

Amphipods 34,500 ft (10,500 m)

Most sea creatures take their oxygen not from the air, but from the water around them. Animals, including sea urchins and shrimplike amphipods, can live in the deepest parts of the ocean.

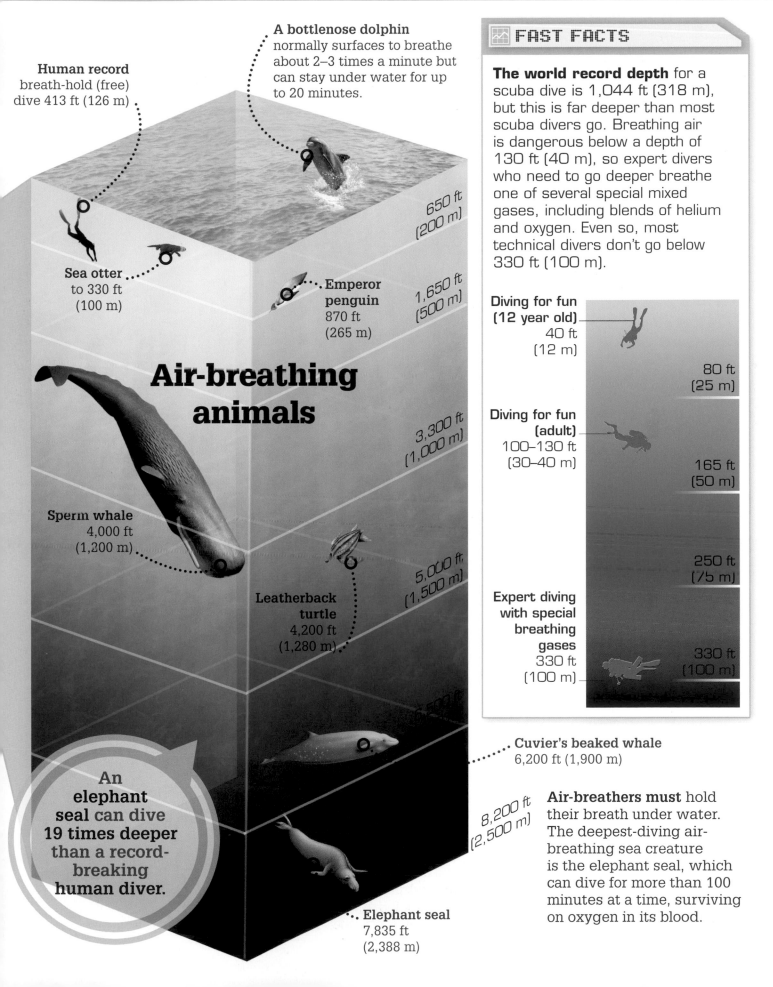

A bottlenose dolphin normally surfaces to breathe about 2–3 times a minute but can stay under water for up to 20 minutes.

Human record breath-hold (free) dive 413 ft (126 m)

Sea otter to 330 ft (100 m)

Emperor penguin 870 ft (265 m)

650 ft (200 m)

1,650 ft (500 m)

Air-breathing animals

3,300 ft (1,000 m)

Sperm whale 4,000 ft (1,200 m)

Leatherback turtle 4,200 ft (1,280 m)

5,000 ft (1,500 m)

An elephant seal can dive 19 times deeper than a record-breaking human diver.

Cuvier's beaked whale 6,200 ft (1,900 m)

8,200 ft (2,500 m)

Elephant seal 7,835 ft (2,388 m)

FAST FACTS

The world record depth for a scuba dive is 1,044 ft (318 m), but this is far deeper than most scuba divers go. Breathing air is dangerous below a depth of 130 ft (40 m), so expert divers who need to go deeper breathe one of several special mixed gases, including blends of helium and oxygen. Even so, most technical divers don't go below 330 ft (100 m).

Diving for fun (12 year old) 40 ft (12 m)

80 ft (25 m)

Diving for fun (adult) 100–130 ft (30–40 m)

165 ft (50 m)

250 ft (75 m)

Expert diving with special breathing gases 330 ft (100 m)

330 ft (100 m)

Air-breathers must hold their breath under water. The deepest-diving air-breathing sea creature is the elephant seal, which can dive for more than 100 minutes at a time, surviving on oxygen in its blood.

How strong is an ant?

An **average-sized ant**, weighing about **0.0001 oz** (0.003 g), is able to **lift** an object that weighs **0.005 oz** (0.15 g)—that's **50 times** its own weight.

If a **man** were as **strong** as an **ant**, he would be able to **lift three cars.**

An ant carries objects in its mandibles—powerful jaws that it also uses to cut, crush, fight, and dig.

This leaf-cutter ant is ¼ in (0.75 cm) long and is able to carry a piece of bark much larger than itself.

LEOPARD STRENGTH

When a leopard kills large prey, such as an antelope, it drags the body up a tree, away from hyenas and other scavengers. A male leopard can drag prey three times its weight—even a small giraffe— to a height of 20 ft (6 m).

Ants are strong because their muscles are bigger relative to the ant's overall size. Physics explains that an ant twice as long would have muscles four times stronger, but a body eight times heavier. This would make the muscles—and the ant— effectively half as strong.

If a man weighing 176 lb (80 kg) could lift 50 times his own weight that would be 4.4 tons (4 metric tons)— the same as three cars.

FAST FACTS

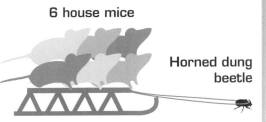

6 house mice

Horned dung beetle

The male horned dung beetle deals with rival males by pushing them out of its burrow. Tests have shown that this species can pull 1,141 times its own body weight—the same as pulling six 0.7-oz (20-g) house mice.

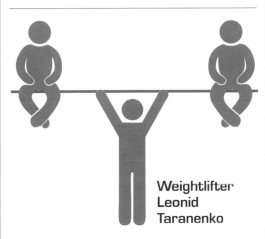

Weightlifter Leonid Taranenko

The largest weight lifted by a human is 586 lb (266 kg). This was achieved by Leonid Taranenko of Russia in 1988 and was nearly twice his body weight. The women's weight-lifting record belongs to Meng Suping of China, who lifted 414 lb (188 kg) in 2012.

Animal data

L O N G MIGRATIONS

6,000 MILES
(9,700 KM)

Leatherback turtles regularly swim **6,000 miles** (9,700 km) each way across the Pacific Ocean between their main feeding sites in California and their breeding areas in Indonesia.

3,000–4,500 MILES
(5,000–7,000 KM)

Eels in Europe have to travel **3,000–4,500 miles** (5,000–7,000 km) to their breeding grounds in the Sargasso Sea.

2,000 MILES
(3,200 KM)

Each year, **monarch butterflies** fly on average **2,000 miles** (3,200 km) between southern California and Mexico.

BIG MIGRATIONS

Every year on Africa's Serengeti Plains more than **1.5 million wildebeest** undertake an **1,800-mile** (2,900-km) round trip on the search for fresh grass. Around **250,000**, or **17%**, don't survive.

17%

Africa's biggest migration takes place each fall when around **8 million fruit bats** fly from the Democratic Republic of the Congo to neighboring Zambia to feast on newly ripened fruit.

SENSITIVE ANIMALS

▶ **Great white sharks** can detect blood in the water from up to **3 miles** (5 km) away. It's been estimated that they can smell a **single drop of blood** in

26 gallons
(100 liters) of water.

▶ **Jewel beetles** have an infrared sensor that allows them to **detect a forest fire** from up to **50 miles** (80 km) away. They then fly

toward the fire

and lay their eggs in the burned tree trunks.

▶ **Seals** have the most sensitive whiskers of any mammal and can **detect a fish** swimming more than **330 ft** (100 m) away.

▶ The heat-sensitive organs of **pit vipers** can detect **temperature** variations of just

0.001°F
(0.002°C).

FLYING FISH

Flying fish can soar over the water for up to **650 ft** (200 m)—the length of two average soccer fields.

KILLER CREATURES

s The sting of a **box jellyfish** is nearly always fatal unless treated immediately. Stings have killed more than **5,500 people** in the past 60 years.

s The venom of a **king cobra** can kill an adult human in **15–30 minutes**.

s A drop of venom from the **marbled cone snail** can kill **20 humans**, or one elephant.

FASTEST FLAPPERS

Some species of **hummingbird** can flap their wings at up to **80 times a second—** so *fast* it produces a faint humming sound.

HOW SNAKES M O V E

All snakes slide along the ground, but not all move in quite the same way. They have a few main ways of getting around on land:

ACCORDION

SERPENTINE

SIDEWINDING

SLOWEST ANIMALS

While a **cheetah** may be able to race at up to **70 mph** (110 kph), some other creatures prefer to take their time getting from A to B.

SEAHORSE
0.1 MPH
(0.15 KPH)

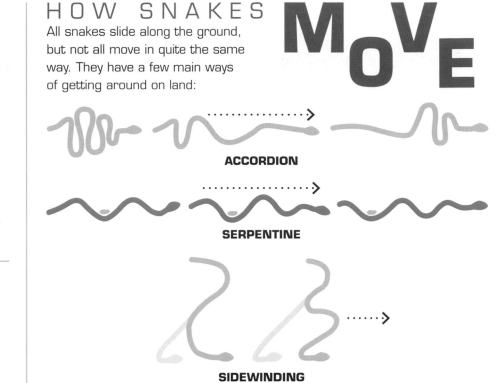

GIANT TORTOISE
0.2 MPH
(0.3 KPH)

GARDEN SNAIL
0.3 MPH
(0.5 KPH)

20 FT (6 M)

650 FT (200 M)

They can stay in the air for up to **45 seconds**, traveling at around **45 mph** (70 kph) and reaching heights of **20 ft** (6 m).

Feats of engineering

People are inventive and are always creating new things. Engineering—designing and making things—has given us powerful rockets, superfast sports cars, spectacularly tall buildings, computers that can do billions of calculations per second—and much more.

One of the greatest engineering feats ever, Dubai's Palm Islands are the biggest manmade islands in the world. Palm Jumeirah (pictured) is shaped like an enormous palm tree, covering an area of 3.1 sq miles (5 sq km)—more than the area of 800 football pitches.

How **fast** is the **fastest car?**

The **fastest cars** in **motor sport** are **top-fuel dragsters**, which reach **330 mph** (530 kph) from a **standing start** in less than **4 seconds.**

112 mph (180 kph)

240 mph (386 kph)

A family car, such as this Ford Focus, can go barely half as fast as a Formula 1 car.

Open-wheeled racing cars can go at speeds up to 231 mph (372 kph) in Formula 1 (above) and more than 240 mph (386 mph) in Indy Car racing.

267.8 mph (431.1 kph)

AMERICAN COMPETITOR

The Hennessey Venom GT is chasing Bugatti's top road-car spot. It holds a world record of 13.63 seconds for acceleration from 0–186 mph (0–300 kph). It has also reached a speed of 266 mph (428 kph), which is only fractionally behind its Italian rival.

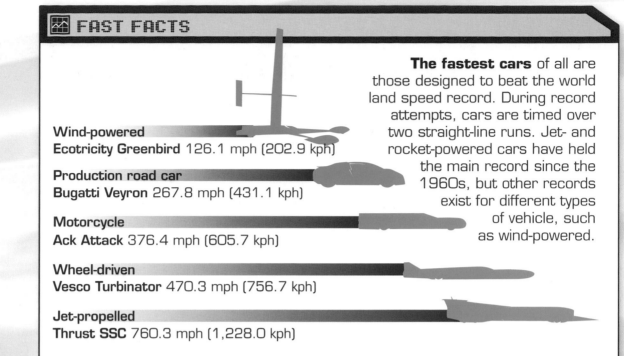

FAST FACTS

The fastest cars of all are those designed to beat the world land speed record. During record attempts, cars are timed over two straight-line runs. Jet- and rocket-powered cars have held the main record since the 1960s, but other records exist for different types of vehicle, such as wind-powered.

Wind-powered
Ecotricity Greenbird 126.1 mph (202.9 kph)

Production road car
Bugatti Veyron 267.8 mph (431.1 kph)

Motorcycle
Ack Attack 376.4 mph (605.7 kph)

Wheel-driven
Vesco Turbinator 470.3 mph (756.7 kph)

Jet-propelled
Thrust SSC 760.3 mph (1,228.0 kph)

"Top fuel" is a class of car used in drag racing. These cars run on a mix of special, high-performance fuels, and race on a strip that is only 1,000–1,320 ft (300–402 m) long. They can accelerate from 0–100 mph (0–160 kph) in less than a second, and have to release parachutes behind them to help them brake.

330 mph (530 kph)

The Bugatti Veyron Super Sport is the fastest production car—that is one built in numbers for people to drive on the road. It can accelerate from 0–60 mph (0–100 kph) in 2.46 seconds.

In races, the **fastest dragsters reach speeds 90 mph (144 kph) greater than** in any Indy Car race.

The *Shanghai Maglev* covers **19 miles (30 km)** in less than **8 minutes**.

STEAM POWER

The first trains were powered by steam. The fastest of all time was the *Mallard*, a British locomotive that reached 126 mph (203 kph).

📊 FAST FACTS

The fastest maglev train speeds have been reached by Japan's maglev test train, the *MLX01*. A manned rocket sled, however, has achieved even faster speeds.

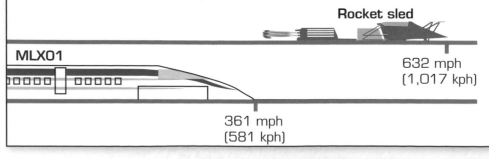

Rocket sled

MLX01

632 mph (1,017 kph)

361 mph (581 kph)

168 mph (270 kph)

The yellow *TGV La Poste* is the world's fastest freight train. It is used to transport mail in and out of Paris, France.

How fast is the fastest train?

The *Shanghai Maglev* is the **fastest passenger train** in the world. It can operate at speeds of up to **267 mph** (430 kph).

China's *Shanghai Maglev Train* is the fastest passenger train in service. Maglevs run on special tracks that lift them off the ground. They are smoother and quieter than ordinary trains.

200 mph (320 kph)

267 mph (430 kph)

The French *TGV* is the world's fastest wheel-based passenger train. It runs on high-speed tracks at up to 200 mph (320 kph) on regular services. A specially adapted version, the *TGV V150*, currently holds the world speed record of 357 mph (575 kph).

The track is called a guideway. When an electric current is sent through the guideway, magnets under the train generate a force that lifts the train and propels itat high speed.

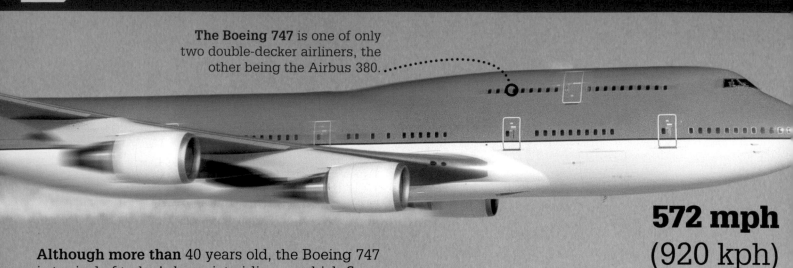

The **Boeing 747** is one of only two double-decker airliners, the other being the Airbus 380.

572 mph
(920 kph)

Although more than 40 years old, the Boeing 747 is typical of today's large jet airliners, which fly passengers at an average speed of 545 mph (877 kph) to a top speed of 572 mph (920 kph).

The Concorde was the fastest-ever passenger jet. It was capable of flying from New York to London in less than 3 hours.

1,354 mph
(2,179 kph)

How **fast** is the **fastest aircraft?**

The **X-15** was the fastest **manned airplane** ever to fly. Its **record speed** of **4,534 mph** (7,297 kph) was set in **1967** and has never been beaten.

FAST FACTS

Flyer
30 mph (48 kph)

Mallard duck
65 mph (105 kph)

4,534 mph (7,297 kph)
X-15—fastest manned aircraft

2,600 mph (4,184 kph)
SpaceShipTwo—fastest passenger spaceplane

2,193 mph (3,529 kph)
SR–71 Blackbird—fastest jet aircraft

700 mph (1,126 kph)
Cessna Citation X—fastest passenger jet

249 mph (400 kph)
Westland Lynx—fastest helicopter

The first aircraft to fly, the Wright brothers' *Flyer*, reached a top speed of 30 mph (48 kph). This is less than half the speed of a mallard duck, which flies at 65 mph (105 kph).

The fastest aircraft fly to the edge of space. Tourists may soon travel there in supersonic space planes.

The X-15 flew at nearly eight times the speed of a Boeing 747.

Bullet speeds vary, but a bullet from an M16 rifle is quicker than the fastest fighter jets.

2,125 mph (3,420 kph)

HTV-2

In 2011, an experimental plane, the unmanned HTV-2, reached a speed of 13,000 mph (21,000 kph)—fast enough to travel from London to Sydney, Australia, in under an hour.

The X-15 couldn't take off like an ordinary plane. The experimental aircraft was carried by a bomber to its cruising altitude. Only then did the X-15 fire up its rocket engines.

4,534 mph (7,297 kph)

The LZ-130 Graf Zeppelin II could carry up to 72 passengers, plus a 40-man crew. With a top speed of 81 mph (131 kph), it had a range of 10,250 miles (16,500 km). The airship was filled with lighter-than-air gas and built to carry passengers across the Atlantic.

The **biggest Zeppelins were 3 times longer and 6 times wider than a Jumbo Jet.**

Graf Zeppelin

AIRBUS BELUGA

The Airbus Beluga is designed to carry large or awkwardly shaped cargo. This includes the parts for Airbus airliners, which are made in four different countries and then airlifted for assembly.

The control gondola contained separate control and observation rooms, plus a central navigation area.

Huge windows, which could be opened during flights, ran the length of the passenger decks.

What was the biggest aircraft?

At **804 ft** (245 m) **long**, the **Zeppelin airships** *Graf Zeppelin II* and *Hindenburg*, built in Germany in the 1930s, were the **largest aircraft** ever to take to the skies.

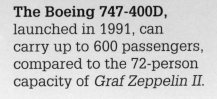

The Boeing 747-400D, launched in 1991, can carry up to 600 passengers, compared to the 72-person capacity of *Graf Zeppelin II*.

Each of the four engine cars were manned by a mechanic at all times during flights.

📊 FAST FACTS

Airbus A380
238.6 ft 8 in (72.72 m)

Boeing 747-8 Intercontinental
250 ft 3 in (76.25 m)

Antonov An-225
275 ft 8 in (84 m)

The Antonov An-225 is the world's longest airplane—longer than the Airbus 380 and the Boeing 747. Designed to carry *Buran*, the Russian Space Shuttle, on its back, it now finds work transporting outsized cargo items.

How fast is the fastest watercraft?

A record of **318 mph** (511 kph) was set by a **speedboat**, the *Spirit of Australia*, in 1978. It has yet to be broken.

The *Spirit of Australia* is five times faster than *Hydroptère*.

FAST FACTS

Sometimes you can go almost as fast on a board as you can on a boat. The kitesurfing record of 64 mph (103 kph) is close behind the fastest sailing craft, *Sailrocket 2*, and is faster than *Hydroptére*'s 59 mph (95 kph). The fastest windsurfer is almost as fast.

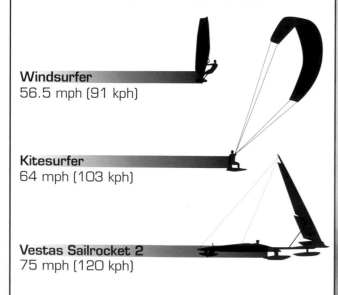

Windsurfer
56.5 mph (91 kph)

Kitesurfer
64 mph (103 kph)

Vestas Sailrocket 2
75 mph (120 kph)

Under each side float of *Hydroptère* is a foil, or wing. Once the boat is at a certain speed, the foils lift it so that it almost flies above the water.

The personal watercraft, or water scooter, is one of the fastest vehicles on water. Its small size, fast speed, and ease of use make it ideal for use by police, lifeguards, and fun seekers.

l'Hydroptère

67 mph (108 kph)

Hydroptère is one of the fastest sailing vessels ever made. The boat is built for speed and its crew is aiming to break sailing world speed records.

l Hydroptère

59 mph (95 kph)

The Spirit of Australia was a jet-powered speed boat driven by Australian Ken Warby.

SPIRIT OF AUSTRALIA
THE WORLDS FASTEST BOAT

318 mph (511 kph)

FOSSEYS

KW2N

FAST FACTS

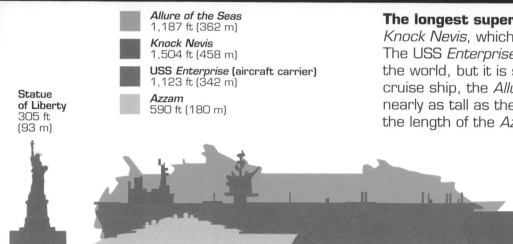

Allure of the Seas
1,187 ft (362 m)

Knock Nevis
1,504 ft (458 m)

USS Enterprise (aircraft carrier)
1,123 ft (342 m)

Azzam
590 ft (180 m)

Statue
of Liberty
305 ft
(93 m)

The longest supertanker ever was the *Knock Nevis*, which was broken up in 2010. The USS *Enterprise* is the longest naval ship in the world, but it is still shorter than the largest cruise ship, the *Allure of the Seas*. The *Alllure* is nearly as tall as the Statue of Liberty, and twice the length of the *Azzam*, the largest private yacht.

How **big** is a **supertanker?**

The
TI Oceania is
the same **length**
as **29 yellow
school buses**
placed end
to end.

The *Oceania* and its three sister ships are the largest ever tankers to have double hulls—the bottom and sides of the ship have two watertight walls to prevent oil spills in the event of an accident.

The world's biggest cruise ship, the *Allure of the Seas,* can carry up to 6,318 passengers and 2,384 crew. Cruise ships are like floating towns, with movie theaters, restaurants, stores, and swimming pools. The *Allure's* park has 12,000 plants.

The ***Knock Nevis's* anchor** weighed 40 tons (36 metric tons)—more than seven African bull elephants. It is the only part of the ship that remains.

At **1,246 ft** (380 m) **long** and **223 ft** (68 m) **wide**, the *TI Oceania* is the **biggest supertanker** afloat today. It can carry **3 million barrels** of **oil**, and when full it **weighs 486,764 tons** (441,585 metric tons).

TI Oceania has a top speed of 16.5 knots (19 mph/31 kph). At this speed it would take 46 seconds for the entire ship to pass someone watching from the shore.

TI OCEANIA

Protective red paint indicates the area of the hull that lies below the water when the supertanker is fully laden.

How much can a ship carry?

The **biggest container ship**, Maersk's *Triple-E*, can carry **18,000** standard **containers**. It is **1,312 ft (400 m) long**.

The bridge (from where the captain controls the ship) sits far forward so containers can be stacked high without the captain losing visibility

MAERSK LINE

Fully loaded, *Triple-E* could carry **36,000 cars** or **863 million cans of soup**.

Standard containers are used to transport all kinds of goods all over the world, from fruit to clothes and TVs. Each standard container is 20 ft (6.1 m) long and 8 ft (2.44 m) wide, and can be lifted from the ship to fit directly onto a lorry or train.

📈 FAST FACTS

The biggest tankers can carry even more cargo than container ships. The *Knock Nevis* supertanker was 1,504 ft (458 m) long and could hold 4.1 million barrels of oil—enough to fill 260 Olympic swimming pools.

Knock Nevis

x 260

Olympic swimming pool

BLUE MARLIN

Heavy-lift ships, such as the *Blue Marlin*, transport huge structures such as oil rigs or aircraft carriers. The ship can submerge its deck to duck under the structure, then raise it again with the cargo on its back.

If all 18,000 containers were loaded onto a single train, the train would be 68 miles (110 km) long.

MAERSK

The ship's hull is covered with enough paint to fill nearly 2.9 million soda cans.

The *Triple-E* is made from enough steel to build 168 Eiffel Towers. It is as tall as a 25-story building, 13 times longer than a blue whale, and 7 buses could park end-to-end across its width. It's too big to enter any port in the Americas, but travels between Europe and Asia.

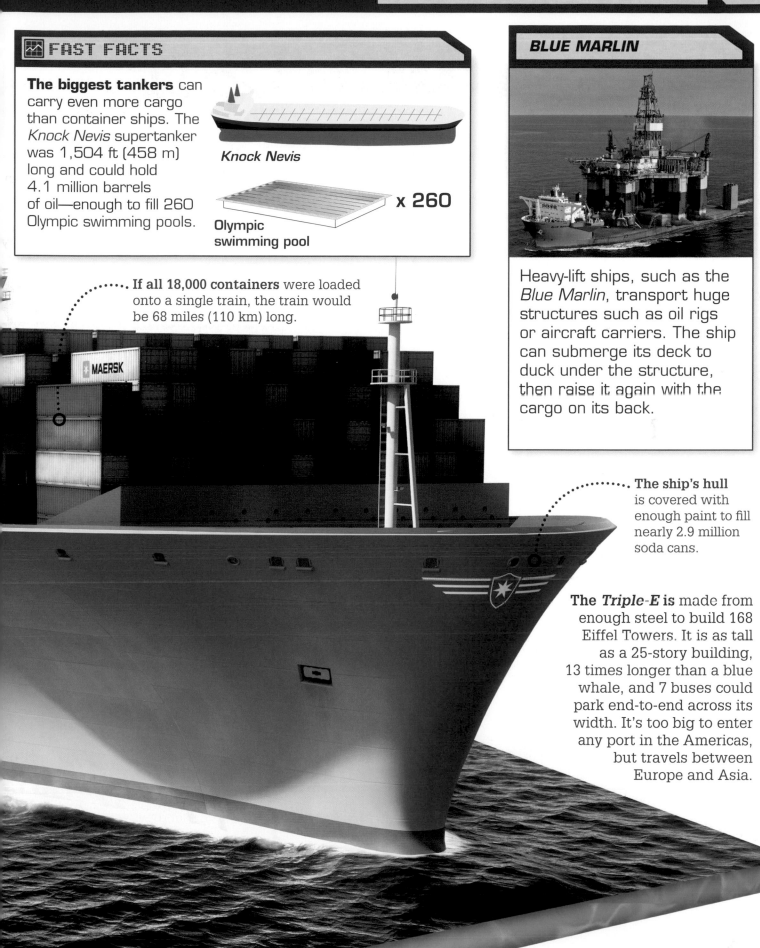

How powerful was the Space Shuttle?

The **Shuttle's** three engines and two rocket boosters produced **6.8 million lb** (3.1 million kg) of **thrust**.

Fuel tank full of liquid hydrogen and liquid oxygen.

Two solid rocket boosters provided 71 percent of the thrust needed for liftoff.

USA

Atlantis

The temperature inside the Shuttle's engines reached 6,000°F (3,315°C).

📈 FAST FACTS

The Space Shuttle's three engines could burn the equivalent of 2.4 swimming pools of liquid fuel in a minute—that's 1,000 gallons (3,785 liters) a second.

Swimming pool
33 x 20 ft (10 x 6 m)

Space Shuttle

Thrust SSC

The Space Shuttle took just under 40 seconds to reach a speed of 620 mph (1,000 kph). However, the holder of the world land-speed record, the *Thrust SSC* rocket car, reached this speed in 16 seconds—less than half the time taken by the Shuttle.

The **Space Shuttle** had the **same power** as **31 Jumbo Jets.**

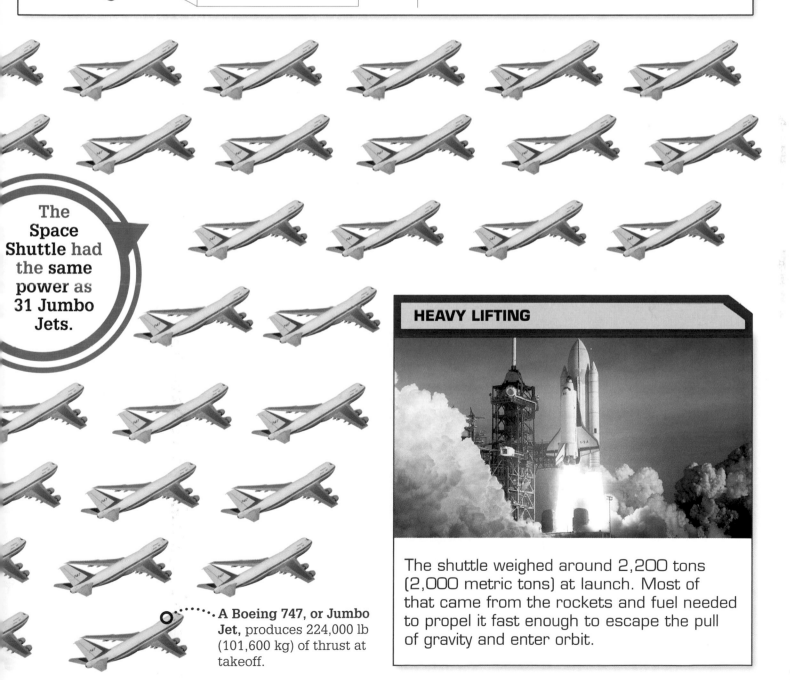

HEAVY LIFTING

The shuttle weighed around 2,200 tons (2,000 metric tons) at launch. Most of that came from the rockets and fuel needed to propel it fast enough to escape the pull of gravity and enter orbit.

A Boeing 747, or Jumbo Jet, produces 224,000 lb (101,600 kg) of thrust at takeoff.

How far have people been into space?

In **1970**, the crew members of the **Apollo 13 Moon mission** traveled a record distance of **248,655 miles (400,171 km) from Earth.**

3. A few hours before splashdown, the Service Module was detached and the crew saw for the first time the huge damage that had been caused by the explosion.

4. The Command Module reentered the Earth's atmosphere at a speed of 24,689 mph (39,733 kph).

The Lunar Module is the part of the spacecraft designed to detach in Moon orbit and descend to the Moon's surface.

The Command Module is where the crew sits during the journey to the Moon.

The Service Module contained a rocket motor, fuel, oxygen, and the electrical power supply.

🖾 FAST FACTS

Voyager 1 is the farthest-flung human-built object in space. It is 11.3 billion miles (18.2 billion km) from Earth, and is about to become the first craft to leave our solar system.

Solar system

Saturn Uranus Neptune

Pluto

Earth **Distance**
Solar system distances are measured in AU (Astronomical Units). One AU is the distance between the Earth and the Sun.

Apollo 13's mission was to orbit the Moon 69 miles (111 km) from its surface, traveling the same distance as previous Apollo Moon missions. Some crew members were going to land on the Moon's surface. When an explosion disabled the spacecraft, however, the mission changed. The spacecraft had to be sent on a new, longer path around the Moon, just to get the crew home safely.

2. Apollo 13 flew 164 miles (264 km) past the Moon before swinging back on its return path.

The **distance from Earth reached by Apollo 13 is equivalent to 10 circuits of Earth's equator.**

1. The craft was 204,000 miles (329,000 km) from Earth and 55 hours into its flight when an explosion crippled the Service Module's fuel, power, and oxygen supplies. The mission to land on the Moon had to be aborted.

MISSION CONTROL

In the Apollo 13 Service Module, a fan in an oxygen tank short-circuited, causing the tank to catch fire and explode. Mission controllers on Earth worked out that they could use the Moon's gravity to bring the craft back on course for home.

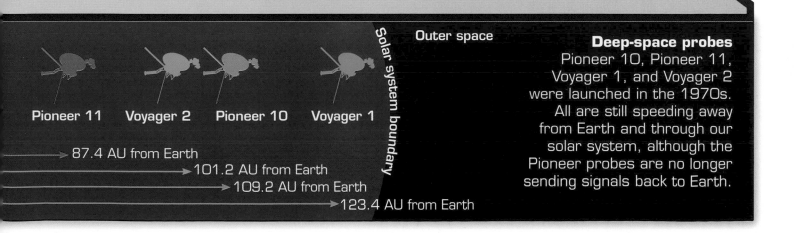

Outer space

Solar system boundary

Deep-space probes
Pioneer 10, Pioneer 11, Voyager 1, and Voyager 2 were launched in the 1970s. All are still speeding away from Earth and through our solar system, although the Pioneer probes are no longer sending signals back to Earth.

Pioneer 11   Voyager 2   Pioneer 10   Voyager 1

87.4 AU from Earth

101.2 AU from Earth

109.2 AU from Earth

123.4 AU from Earth

How **high** was the **highest** parachute jump?

In 2012, Austrian **Felix Baumgartner leapt** from a balloon nearly **128,000 ft** (39,000 m) above the Earth.

At the edge of space, the air pressure is less than 2 percent of what it is at sea level. Baumgartner wore a pressurized suit to prevent him from blacking out as he fell.

Wispy cirrus clouds can form as high as 46,000 ft (14,000 m).

The **skydive** was roughly **four times** the **height of** a crusing airliner.

Airliners usually cruise at around 33,000 ft (10,000 m).

Most parachute jumps are made from under 14,000 ft (4,300 m). Even at this height, you will freefall at around 100 mph (160 kph).

BREAKING THE SOUND BARRIER

During freefall Baumgartner reached a speed of 844 mph (1,358 kph), becoming the first person to break the sound barrier without the help of a vehicle.

Baumgartner traveled to a height of 127,852 ft (38,969 m) in a balloon before jumping from the capsule.

Jumping from the stratosphere is very risky. The air is far too thin to breath, but Baumgartner could only carry a 10-minute supply of air with him for the descent. The lack of air pressure also made it hard for him to stop from spinning as he fell. Luckily, he managed to pull himself into a correct freefall position.

The stratosphere lies above the troposphere, to an altitude of 160,000 ft (50,000 m).

The troposphere, the lowest layer of the atmosphere where most cloud and weather occurs, ends at 40,000 ft (12,000 m).

At 110,000 ft (33,500 m) Baumgartner broke the sound barrier.

At 4,900 ft (1,500 m) above the ground, Baumgartner opened his parachute and landed safely on the ground.

FAST FACTS

Only rocket planes are able to fly high in the atmosphere because the lack of oxygen prevents jet engines from working.

International Space Station 1,161,400 ft (354,000 m)

Passenger spacecraft SpaceShipTwo 359,000 ft (110,000 m)

Highest rocket airplane X-15 354,200 ft (108,000 m)

Highest jet airplane SR-71 Blackbird 80,000 ft (24,000 m)

Passenger airliner 33,000 ft (10,000 m)

Vehicle data

ON AND ON AND ON

A Volvo car built in 1966 had by 2012 driven
2.9 million miles
(4.7 million km)—that's the equivalent of almost **117 times** around the globe.

WORLD'S BIGGEST

Tunnel boring machine
With a diameter of **63 ft** (19.25 m) and a weight of **4,200 tons** (3,800 metric tons), this mighty machine is being used to dig a new road tunnel beneath St. Petersburg, Russia.

Propeller
Measuring **31 ft** (9.6 m) across and weighing **143 tons** (130 metric tons), it is used to drive the *Emma Maersk*, one of the world's biggest container ships.

DOWN DEEP

1,043 ft (318 m) Deepest scuba dive

2,001 ft (610 m) Deepest dive in an atmospheric diving suit

1,608 ft (490 m) Operating depth of the nuclear submarine USS *Seawolf*

14,800 ft (4,500 m) Maximum diving depth of the US Navy manned submersible *Alvin*

Deepsea Challenger

Trieste

36,200 ft (11,030 m) Challenger Deep, the deepest point, has been visited twice: in 1960 by the submersible *Trieste*; and in 2012 by *Deepsea Challenger*.

LONGEST NONSTOP PASSENGER FLIGHTS

Sydney, Australia to Dallas-Fort Worth, Texas: **8,577 miles** (13,804 km)　**15 HOURS, 25 MINUTES**

Johannesburg, South Africa to Atlanta, Georgia: **8,439 miles** (13,582 km)　**17 HOURS**

LONGEST TRAIN

- The world's longest train had **682 cars** and eight locomotives. It was used just once, to haul iron ore in Australia in 2001, and it measured **4.57 miles** (7.353 km) long. That's the length of **8.8 Burj Khalifas**, laid end to end.

- The longest ever passenger train ran in Australia in 2004. It was **0.75 miles** (1.2 km) long and was made up of two locomotives and **43 cars**.

TOTAL AMOUNT OF RAILROAD TRACK IN THE WORLD

770,262 miles (1,239,615 km)—over three times the distance from Earth to the Moon.

The three countries with the most railroad track are the US, Russia, and China. Among them, they have just under a third of all the world's track.

US: **139,679 miles** (224,792 km)

Russia: **54,157 miles** (87,157 km)

China: **53,400 miles** (86,000 km)

Land vehicle

An enormous excavator used in the German mining industry, the **Bagger 288** is **722 ft** (220 m) long, **311 ft** (95 m) high, and weighs **45,500 tons** (41,300 metric tons). It can fill 2,400 coal wagons a day.

Human

Animal

The blue whale measures **100 ft** (30 m) long.

How **small** is the **tiniest** computer?

A **computer** with a **pressure sensor**, a **microprocessor**, **memory**, a **battery**, a **solar cell**, and a **wireless radio** measures just **0.04 in** (1 mm) square. It is designed to be be **implanted** in patients' **eyes**.

Computers are getting smaller each year. In 1993, to do 143 GFLOPS (143 billion calculations a second) you needed a computer 5 ft (1.5 m) tall and 25 ft (8 m) long. In 2013 just four laptops exceed this performance.

Moore's Law, invented by Gordon Moore, a founder of Intel, suggests that computers double in perfomance every two years. In fact, the average speed of the 500 fastest computers in the world more than doubled every two years in the decade 2002–2012.

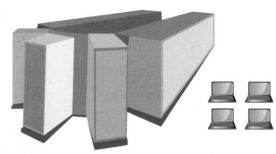

Intel Paragon
supercomputer, 1993
143 GFLOPS

4 Intel i5 laptop
processors, 2013
45 GFLOPS each

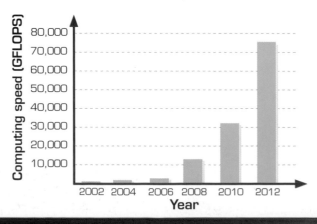

Computing speed (GFLOPS)

80,000
70,000
60,000
50,000
40,000
30,000
20,000
10,000

2002 2004 2006 2008 2010 2012
Year

This minuscule device is made to sit inside the eye of someone suffering from the eye disease glaucoma. It records pressure inside the eye and sends the data, with its radio, to a conventional computer outside. Devices similar to this could soon be implanted throughout the body and could do a wide range of jobs.

The components of the computer include a thin film battery that can be charged by 1.5 hours of sunlight hitting a tiny solar cell. The device can store a week's worth of data.

Five of these miniature computers would fit across this fingertip.

MICROPROCESSORS

Computers became a lot smaller in 1971 with the invention of the microprocessor—the silicon chip that is the central processing unit of a computer. A silicon chip has a miniature electrical circuit printed on it. These printed circuits are smaller every year.

How **many books** can you **fit** on a **flash drive?**

A **1-terabyte (TB)** flash drive can store the text of **1 million books**. One terabyte is just over **1 million megabytes** (MB), or more than **1 trillion bytes.**

A flash drive weighs less than 1.1 oz (30 g) but can hold 1 TB of data. Flash memory can be erased and reprogrammed thousands of times.

A 1-TB flash drive could store **1 million 200-page books.**

ATOMIC DATA STORAGE

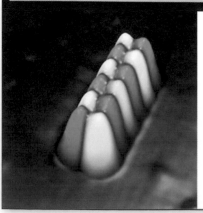

Seen here under a powerful electron microscope is the world's smallest data storage unit. Scientists have used just 12 iron atoms to hold one bit (the basic unit of information), and 96 atoms to hold a byte. A hard disk still needs half a billion atoms per byte.

FAST FACTS

The Library of Congress in Washington, D.C., is the biggest library in the world, containing 35 million books. All the text in those books could be stored on nine 4-TB hard disks.

Storage media are getting more sophisticated every few years. Each piece of new technology stores many times more data than the previous one. They are also becoming faster and, because they have no moving parts, smaller and more durable.

36-TB

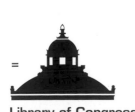

= **Library of Congress**

3.5" floppy disk 1.44 MB

Zip disk 100 MB

CD 700 MB

DVD 4.7 GB

Dual-layer Blu-ray disk 50 GB

2-TB Flash drive 2 TB

Computer data

SOCIAL **NETWORKS**

In 2007, fewer than **500 million** people around the world used social networking sites, such as Facebook. Over the next 5 years, this figure grew to more than

1.2 BILLION—more than 82% of the world's online population.

VIDEO GAME DEVELOPMENT
COST$

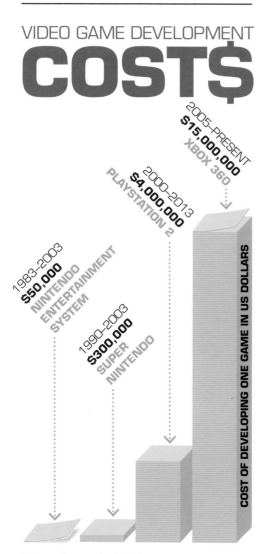

1983–2003
$50,000
NINTENDO ENTERTAINMENT SYSTEM

1990–2003
$300,000
SUPER NINTENDO

2000–2013
$4,000,000
PLAYSTATION 2

2005–PRESENT
$15,000,000
XBOX 360

COST OF DEVELOPING ONE GAME IN US DOLLARS

Since the early 1980s, the **average cost of developing a video game** has increased by more than

30,000%.

COMPUTER MEMORY
GROWTH

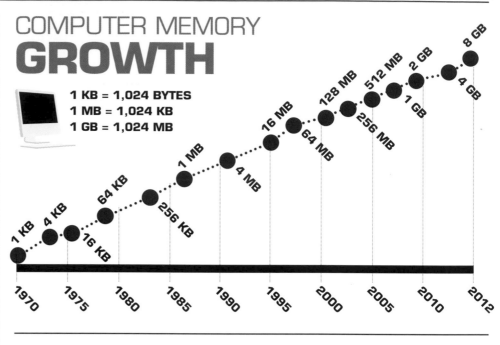

1 KB = 1,024 BYTES
1 MB = 1,024 KB
1 GB = 1,024 MB

1 KB · 4 KB · 16 KB · 64 KB · 256 KB · 1 MB · 4 MB · 16 MB · 64 MB · 128 MB · 256 MB · 512 MB · 1 GB · 2 GB · 4 GB · 8 GB

1970 · 1975 · 1980 · 1985 · 1990 · 1995 · 2000 · 2005 · 2010 · 2012

SUPER
COMPUTER

The world's **fastest computer**, the **Cray Titan**, uses **8,000 kW** of electricity when it is running at full speed. That's equivalent to **1 million** energy-saving 8-watt **lightbulbs**.

PERCENTAGE OF **PEOPLE ONLINE** IN EACH CONTINENT IN 2012

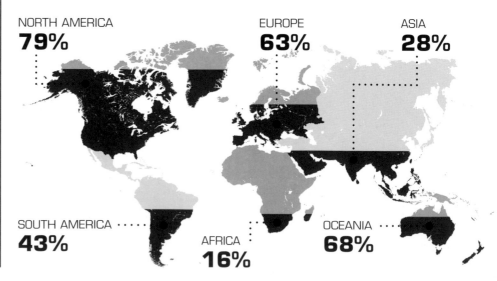

NORTH AMERICA
79%

EUROPE
63%

ASIA
28%

SOUTH AMERICA
43%

AFRICA
16%

OCEANIA
68%

FLOOR SPACE

ENIAC, the world's **first electronic computer**, was built in 1946. It covered **1,798 sq ft** (167 sq m), and could perform

10,000 calculations per second.

Today's fastest computer, **Titan**, covers **4,349 sq ft** (404 sq m), and performs

20,000 trillion

calculations per second.

MOON LANDING

The **computer** on board the **Apollo 11** spacecraft that landed on the Moon in 1969 had just **72 kb** of memory, of which just **2 kb** was RAM.

WEBSITE GROWTH

Since 1991, the number of websites has grown from 1 to more than 660 million.

FIRST WEBSITE:
http://info.cern.ch
August 6, 1991

700,000,000
600,000,000
500,000,000
400,000,000
300,000,000
200,000,000
100,000,000
0

1990   1995   2000   2005   2010   2012

@ YOU'VE GOT MAIL

The **first email** was sent by computer engineer Ray Tomlinson in Cambridge, Massachusetts, in **1971**.

E-BOOK GROWTH

Percentage of book sales in the US, the world's biggest book market, that were e-books

2002: **0.05%**	2009: **3.17%**		
2006: **0.50%**	2011: **16.97%**		
2008: **1.18%**	2012: **22.55%**		

In 2012, online booksellers reported that e-books were outselling paper books for the first time.

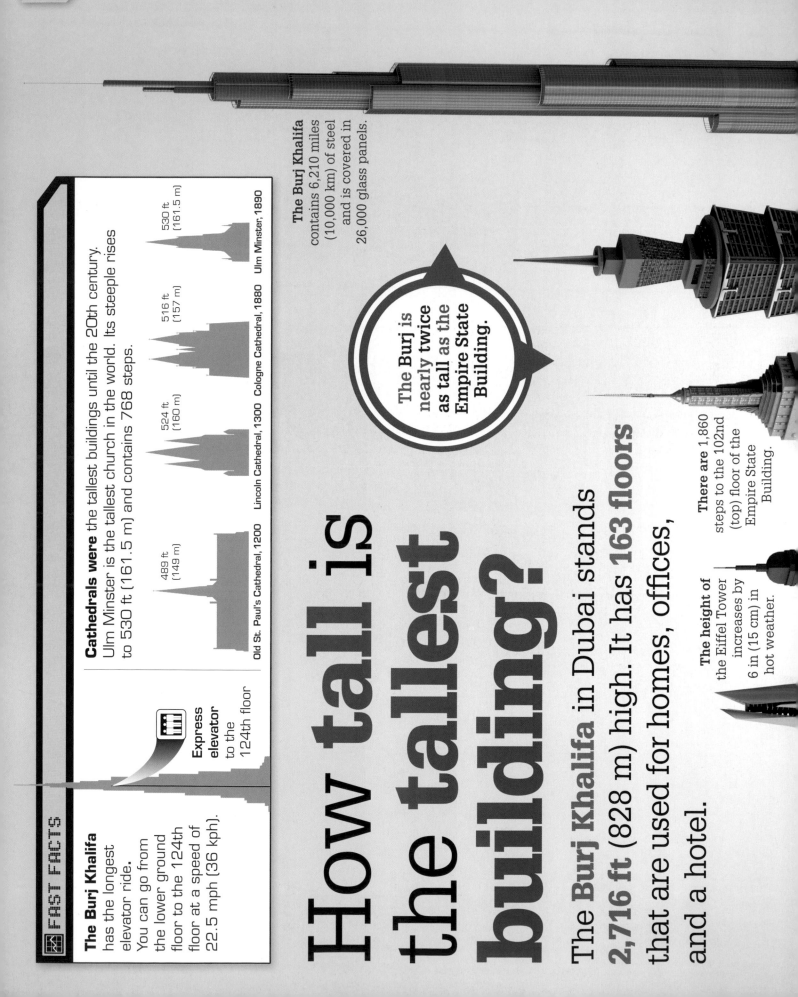

How tall is the tallest building?

The **Burj Khalifa** in Dubai stands **2,716 ft (828 m)** high. It has **163 floors** that are used for homes, offices, and a hotel.

The **Burj Khalifa** contains 6,210 miles (10,000 km) of steel and is covered in 26,000 glass panels.

The Burj is nearly twice as tall as the Empire State Building.

There are 1,860 steps to the 102nd (top) floor of the Empire State Building.

The height of the Eiffel Tower increases by 6 in (15 cm) in hot weather.

The Burj Khalifa has the longest elevator ride. You can go from the lower ground floor to the 124th floor at a speed of 22.5 mph (36 kph).

Express elevator to the 124th floor

Cathedrals were the tallest buildings until the 20th century. Ulm Minster is the tallest church in the world. Its steeple rises to 530 ft (161.5 m) and contains 768 steps.

489 ft (149 m)
Old St. Paul's Cathedral, 1200

524 ft (160 m)
Lincoln Cathedral, 1300

516 ft (157 m)
Cologne Cathedral, 1880

530 ft (161.5 m)
Ulm Minster, 1890

The Shard is the tallest building in Western Europe.

Great Pyramid, Giza, Egypt
481 ft (147 m)

Shard, London, UK
1,016 ft (310 m)

Eiffel Tower, Paris, France
1,052 ft (321 m)

Empire State Building, New York City, US
1,453 ft (443 m) to the top of the spire

Taipei Tower, Taipei, Taiwan
1,670 ft (509 m) to the top of the spire

Burj Khalifa, Dubai, UAE
2,716 ft (828 m) to the top of the spire

Record-breaking buildings never hold their records for long. All the structures above were at one time the tallest of their kind. The Burj became the world's tallest building in 2010, but even taller structures are already planned that could reach 3,300 ft (1,000 m) into the sky.

VIEW FROM THE TOP

This is the view from the top of the 700 ft (200 m) spire on the Burj. The spire was built inside the tower and lifted into place. In windy conditions the spire sways by as much as 4 ft (1.2 m).

Around the top of the roof of the London stadium, the lighting towers reach 197 ft (60 m) above the sports area. ......

You could fit **3 London Olympic stadiums** inside the factory walls.

The Boeing 747 is 64 ft (19 m) high and was the biggest aircraft in the world when the factory was built in the 1960s. ......

How **big** is the **biggest** building?

A huge mural on the side of the building covers six doors, each of which is 82 ft (25 m) high and the length of a National Football League (NFL) field.

Used for putting airplanes together, **Boeing's Everett Factory** in Seattle has a **volume** of **472 million cu ft** (13.4 million cu m).

The Everett factory is so huge you could fit the whole of Disneyland or 55 soccer fields inside. Beneath the plant are 2.3 miles (3.7 km) of pedestrian tunnels.

PRODUCTION LINE

This single bay inside the plant is holding 12 airplanes waiting to be painted. The Everett factory can produce eight Boeing 777s and ten 787s a month.

The perimeter of the building measures 2.2 miles (3.5 km).

FAST FACTS

About 160 gallons (600 liters) of paint are applied to each Boeing 747—that is 7.5 bathtubfuls.

The Everett Factory is the biggest building by volume, but others have a larger floor space.

Everett Factory, Seattle
4,280,000 sq ft
(398,000 sq m)

Pentagon, Washington
6.6 million sq ft
(610,000 sq m)

Abraj Al-Bait Towers hotel, Mecca:
17 million sq ft (1,600,000 sq m)

Dubai International Airport,
Terminal 3: 18.44 million sq ft
(1,713,000 sq m)

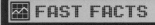

Millau bridge deck
40,000 tons
(36,000 metric tons)

5 x
Eiffel Towers

The bridge's steel deck contains enough to steel to make five Eiffel towers. The deck was built in a total of 2,200 separate sections that were welded together into two halves, then pushed out toward each other from opposite sides of the valley.

Each of the longest cables on the viaduct are strong enough to withstand the thrust of eight Boeing 747 airliners at maximum thrust.

How tall is the tallest bridge?

The Millau Viaduct carries the road from Montpelier, in southern France, to Paris. The bridge is 8,070 ft (2,460 m) long and was opened in 2004.

The **Millau Viaduct**, which spans the valley of the **Tarn River** in **France**, is the **tallest bridge** in the world. Its **largest mast** is **1,125 ft** (343 m) above the base, where it meets the **valley floor**.

The tallest mast is 1,125 ft (343 m) tall. There are seven masts of different heights across the valley. Each holds 11 pairs of stays (metal cables). The stays support the road deck.

The Empire State Building measures 1,250 ft (381 m) to its roof. If it sat in the bottom of the valley, the roof would be just 40 ft (12 m) above the bridge's highest point.

LONGEST BRIDGE

The world's longest bridge is the Danyang–Kunshan Grand Bridge in China, at 102.4 miles (164.8 km) long. The bridge is part of the Beijing–Shanghai High-Speed Railroad. Two more of the world's five longest bridges are part of the same railroad line.

The **Millau Viaduct** is almost as tall as the **Empire State Building.**

How heavy is the Great Pyramid?

Egypt's **Great Pyramid of Giza**, one of Earth's oldest buildings, weighs **5,750,100 tons** (5,216,400 metric tons).

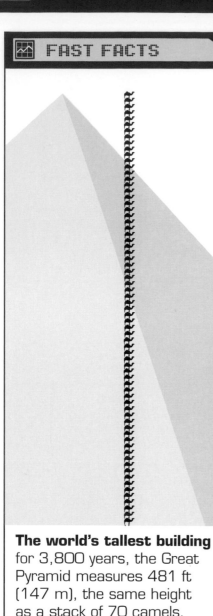

The world's tallest building for 3,800 years, the Great Pyramid measures 481 ft (147 m), the same height as a stack of 70 camels.

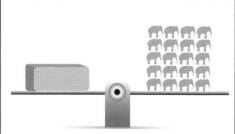

The largest of the 2,300,000 stones that make up the Great Pyramid weigh 69 tons (63 metric tons)—the weight of 20 African bull elephants.

The **Great Pyramid weighs the same as 16 Empire State Buildings.**

The Great Pyramid is a nearly solid construction of limestone measuring 746 ft (227 m) along each side. It was built in about 2560–2540 BCE as a tomb for Pharaoh Khufu.

The Empire State Building has a steel frame covered with concrete and glass. Unlike the pyramid, it isn't solid, being 102 floors of mainly office space.

To the top of its spire, the Empire State Building measures 1,454 ft (443 m) tall. When it was finished in 1931, it was the world's tallest building.

To dig the foundations of the Empire State Building, workers removed soil weighing more than the building itself.

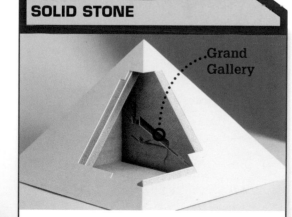

SOLID STONE

Grand Gallery

The Great Pyramid is almost solid stone, except for its small burial chambers and passageways. The biggest of these spaces, the Grand Gallery, is only 7 ft (2 m) wide.

How deep can we dig?

The **deepest ever human-made hole** is the **Kola Superdeep Borehole**, which was begun in 1970. **By 1994**, when the project was abandoned, the hole was more than **7.5 miles** (12 km) **deep**.

The center of the Earth is 3,959 miles (6,371 km) below the surface. A journey there would begin with between 3 and 44 miles (5 and 70 km) of crust. Below this are the fluid rocks of the mantle and the liquid-metal outer core. Each of these layers is more than 1,200 miles (2,000 km) thick. The inner core is 794 miles (1,278 km) across.

The deepest ever man-made hole did **not even break through** the Earth's thinnest, outermost layer—the crust.

Kola Superdeep Borehole (Russia) 7.62 miles (12.262 km)

Mantle

Outer core

Inner core

Crust

Mantle

The boundary between the Earth's crust and mantle in Russia's Kola Peninsula is at a depth of about 22 miles (35 km).

The TauTona elevator travels at 52 ft (16 m) per second but it still takes an hour to take workers to the bottom of the shaft.

TauTona Gold Mine in South Africa is the world's deepest, at 12,800 ft (3,900 m). The mine has about 500 miles (800 km) of tunnels worked by 5,000 miners.

South Africa

TauTona miners are the humans who have traveled deepest into the Earth. The rock face in these lowest passageways can reach 140°F (60°C), so the mine shafts are air-conditioned to a safe temperature.

The Kola borehole project aimed to reach the boundary between the Earth's crust and mantle. Although the borehole penetrated less than a third of the crust, it reached rocks more than 2.5 billion years old.

Russia

FAST FACTS

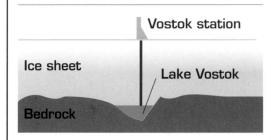

Kola is still the world's deepest borehole, but it is no longer the longest. In 2012, Exxon drilled an oil well 40,593 ft (12,376 m) long. Parts of it run horizontally, however, so it is not quite as deep.

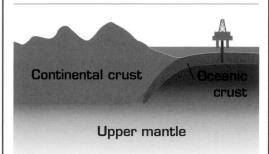

In 1989, Russian scientists began a project to drill through 2 miles (3 km) of Antarctic ice to reach Lake Vostok, a freshwater lake that had lain sealed under the ice for more than 15 million years. In 2012, the scientists reached their goal.

Continental crust · Oceanic crust · Upper mantle

Scientists almost broke through the crust where is it very thin, at less than 3.4 miles (5.5 km), in the ocean off Costa Rica. Oceanic crust is always thinner than continental crust, which forms the Earth's landmasses and is 15–45 miles (25–70 km) thick.

How much gold is there?

From **ancient times** to the **present day**, experts estimate that just **188,800 tons** (171,300 metric tons) of **gold** have been dug out of the ground.

GOLD NUGGETS

A nugget is a naturally occurring lump of gold. Most nuggets are small—but not all of them. This top shelf shows a model of the Welcome Stranger nugget, found in Australia in 1869 and weighing about 173 lb (78 kg).

A tennis court is 78 ft (23.78 m) long.

A ball the width of a tennis court might not sound big enough for 188,800 tons (171,300 metric tons) of gold, but gold is a very heavy metal. Two solid gold house bricks would weigh as much as an adult person.

The ball may look like a lot of gold, but this is all the gold that has ever been mined anywhere on Earth, since the beginning of history. Every day, the world produces enough iron to make more than 40 iron balls the same size!

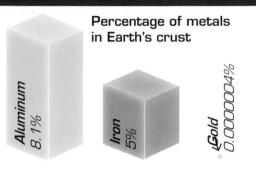

Percentage of metals in Earth's crust

Aluminum 8.1%

Iron 5%

Gold 0.0000004%

Gold is much rarer than iron or aluminum, which make up large percentages of the Earth's crust. Gold is valuable because it is so rare, but also because it never rusts or tarnishes.

Gold left in the ground

Mined Gold

We have already mined about 80 percent of the world's recoverable gold. Only 51,000 tons (46,000 metric tons) of the gold left in the ground could be extracted with existing technology.

All the world's **mined gold** would make **a solid ball 78 ft 9 in (24 m)** across.

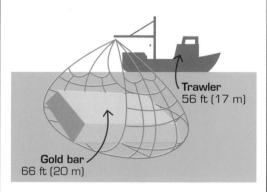

Trawler 56 ft (17 m)

Gold bar 66 ft (20 m)

Seawater contains dissolved gold. There may be up to 16,500 tons (15,000 metric tons) of it in the world's oceans. If this gold could be extracted, it would make a bar measuring 66 ft x 33 ft x 13 ft (20 m x 10 m x 4 m).

Buildings data

BIGGEST CITIES BY POPULATION

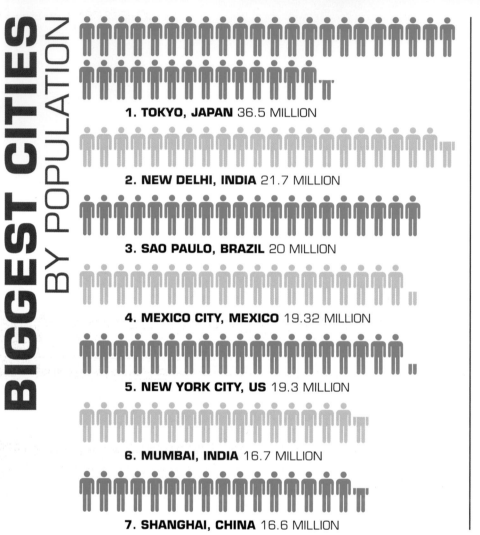

1. TOKYO, JAPAN 36.5 MILLION

2. NEW DELHI, INDIA 21.7 MILLION

3. SAO PAULO, BRAZIL 20 MILLION

4. MEXICO CITY, MEXICO 19.32 MILLION

5. NEW YORK CITY, US 19.3 MILLION

6. MUMBAI, INDIA 16.7 MILLION

7. SHANGHAI, CHINA 16.6 MILLION

FASTEST LIFT

Located in the Shanghai Tower skyscraper in China, it can travel at

3,543 ft

(1,080 m) per minute, or just less than 40 mph (65 kph).

LARGEST DAMS

1 **SYNCRUDE TAILINGS DAM,** CANADA **19 BILLION CU FT** (540 MILLION CU M)

2 **CHAPETÓN,** ARGENTINA **10.5 BILLION CU FT** (296 MILLION CU M)

3 **PATI,** ARGENTINA **8.4 BILLION CU FT** (238 MILLION CU M)

An Olympic swimming pool measures 88,000 cu ft (2,500 cu m), so the Syncrude Dam is the same as 216,000 pools of building material.

WORLD'S L O N G E

WORLD'S MOST **NORTHERLY**

NORTH
ALERT, CANADA:
508 MILES (817 KM)
FROM THE NORTH POLE

SOUTH
**AMUNDSEN-SCOTT
SCIENTIFIC BASE**
AT THE GEOGRAPHIC SOUTH POLE

AND **SOUTHERLY** SETTLEMENTS

LARGEST STORE

Shinsegae Centumcity
Department Store, South Korea.
Spread over **18 floors**, it has an
overall floor area of **3.16 million sq ft**
(293,904 sq m)—that's more than **40**
average-sized **soccer fields**.

LONGEST TUNNELS

LONGEST CONTINUOUS TUNNEL
DELAWARE AQUEDUCT, US
85 MILES (137 KM)

LONGEST UNDERSEA TUNNEL
SEIKAN TUNNEL, JAPAN
34 MILES (54 KM)
∧T **787 FT** (240 M)

LONGEST ROAD TUNNEL
LAERDAL TUNNEL, NORWAY
16 MILES (25 KM)

S T ROAD BRIDGES

1. BANG NA EXPRESSWAY THAILAND
177,000 FT (54,000 M)

2. LAKE PONTCHARTRAIN CAUSEWAY US
126,122 FT (38,442 M)

3. MANCHAC SWAMP BRIDGE US
120,440 FT (36,710 M)

WORLD'S **HIGHEST**

HIGHEST CITY
LA RINCONADA
PERU
16,729 FT
(5,099 M)
ABOVE SEA LEVEL

HIGHEST CAPITAL CITY
LA PAZ
BOLIVIA
11,942 FT
(3,640 M)
ABOVE SEA LEVEL

LOWEST CAPITAL CITY
BAKU
AZERBAIJAN
92 FT
(28 M)
BELOW SEA LEVEL

LOWEST CITY
JERICHO
WEST BANK,
MIDDLE EAST
853 FT
(260 M)
BELOW SEA LEVEL

SEA LEVEL

AND **LOWEST** CITIES

INDEX

ACKNOWLEDGMENTS

Dorling Kindersley would like to thank: Neha Gupta and Samira Sood for proofreading; Helen Peters for indexing; Fran Baines, Carron Brown, Matilda Gollon, Caroline Stamps, and Fleur Star for editorial assistance; Rachael Grady, Mary Sandberg, Jemma Westing, and Jeongeun Yule Park for design assistance; and Simon Holland, Katie John, Martyn Page, and Chris Woodford, for fact-checking.

The publisher would like to thank the following for their kind permission to reproduce their photographs:

(Key: a-above; b-below/bottom; c-center; f-far; l-left; r-right; t-top)

2 Corbis: STScI / NASA (tr). **3 Corbis:** National Geographic Society / Richard Nowitz (tl); Michele Westmorland (tc). **Dreamstime.com:** Pictac (bl); Haider Yousuf (tr). **4-5 Corbis:** STScI / NASA. **6-7 Alan Friedman / avertedimagination.com:** (c). **6 Institute for Solar Physics:** SST / Göran Scharmer / Mats Löfdahl (bl). **7 NASA:** GSFC / F. Espenak (cl/Reproduced five times). **8 NASA:** Hinode / XRT (clb). **9 Dreamstime.com:** Elisanth (cra/Reproduced four times, cr/moons); Stanalin (tr, crb, cr). **10-11 Pascal Henry,www.lesud.com. 10 NASA:** (clb). **12-13 Pascal Henry,www.lesud.com:** (c). **13 NASA:** JPL / Space Science Institute (tc). **14-15 Science Photo Library:** Mark Garlick. **14 Dorling Kindersley:** London Planetarium (fcl). **Dreamstime.com:** Elisanth (cl). **15 NASA:** (bc). **16 Dreamstime.com:** Mmeeds (clb). **18 NASA:** ESA and H. Hammel, MIT (clb). **20 Dreamstime.com:** Jabiru (bl). **25 NASA:** ESA, J. Hester, A. Loll (ASU) (tl). **27 NASA:** CXC / SAO / F. Seward (tc). **29 NASA Goddard Space Flight Center:** Tom Zagwodzki (tr). **31 Corbis:** Visuals Unlimited (cr). **32 NASA:** (bl). **32-33 Science Photo Library:** Chris Butler (c). **33 ESA / Hubble:** S. Beckwith (STScI) and the HUDF Team (br). **Getty Images:** Azem Ramadani (tl). **Science Photo Library:** Mark Garlick (cr). **36-37 Corbis:** National Geographic Society /

Richard Nowitz. **40 Science Photo Library:** Geoeye (bc). **43 NASA:** Visible Earth / Jeff Schmaltz (cr). **45 Dreamstime.com:** Asdf_1 (tc). **46 Dreamstime.com:** Ericsch (bl). **48 Dreamstime.com:** Maxwell De Araújo Rodrigues (cla/Reproduced seven times). **49 Getty Images:** National Geographic (cr). **50 Corbis:** Galen Rowell (bl). **52 NASA:** JPL / University of Arizona (clb). **54 Corbis:** Arctic-Images (clb). **56 Corbis:** Charles & Josette Lenars (bc). **57 Getty Images:** Mike Copeland (crb). **58-59 Getty Images:** National Geographic. **60 Corbis:** Paul Souders (clb). **62 Corbis:** Science Faction / Norbert Wu (clb). **65 Corbis:** Nippon News / Aflo / Newspaper / Mainichi (clb). **66 Getty Images:** Paul Souders (bl). **68 NSIDC:** USGS, W.O. Field (1941) and B. F. Molnia (2004) (clb). **69 Dreamstime.com:** Maxwell De Araújo Rodrigues (cr/Reproduced five times). **72 Getty Images:** Katsumasa Iwasawa (clb). **72-73 Dreamstime.com:** Stockshoppe (c). **73 Dreamstime.com:** Laraslk (crb). **74 Corbis:** Visuals Unlimited (clb). **75 Dreamstime.com:** Pictac (bc). **78 Getty Images:** (bl). **78-79 Getty Images:** Hulton Archive. **80 Corbis:** epa / Michael Reynolds (bl). **82 Corbis:** Ocean (clb). **82-83 Corbis:** Ikon Images / Jurgen Ziewe (c). **84-85 Corbis:** Michele Westmorland. **86 Corbis:** TempSport / Jerome Prevost (cl). Dreamstime.com: Alexandr Mitiuc (clb, bc, br). **86-87 Dorling Kindersley:** Zygote Media Group (c). **87 Dreamstime.com:** Alexandr Mitiuc (bl, bc, crb). **88 Getty Images:** Vince Michaels (br). **Science Photo Library:** GJLP / CNRI (clb). **89 Corbis:** 3d4Medical.com (bl). **90-91 Alamy Images:** D. Hurst. **91 Alamy Images:** AlamyCelebrity (tc). **92 Corbis:** Science Photo Library / Steve Gschmeissner (cl). **96 Corbis:** Visuals Unlimited (clb). **97 Corbis:** Minden Pictures / Flip Nicklin (bc). **Dorling Kindersley:** Natural History Museum, London (bl). **100 Dreamstime.com:** Lindsay Douglas (cl). **100-101 National Geographic Stock:** Michael Nichols (b). **103 naturepl.com:** Doc White (tc). **104 Dorling Kindersley:** Bedrock Studios (tc). Dreamstime.com:

Ibrahimyogurtcu (bc). **104-105 Dorling Kindersley:** Andrew Kerr (c). **106-107 Dorling Kindersley:** Andrew Kerr (c). **107 Dorling Kindersley:** Jon Hughes and Russell Gooday (cr). **108 Science Photo Library:** Peter Chadwick (clb). **110-111 Science Photo Library:** Christian Darkin. **112 Paul Nylander,http://bugman123.com. 113 Alamy Images:** Michal Cerny (tc). **114 Alamy Images:** Louise Murray (clb). **116-117 Dreamstime.com:** Bruce Crandall (c). **118 Alamy Images:** Kevin Elsby (t). **119 Alamy Images:** Rolf Nussbaumer Photography (bl). **Dreamstime.com:** Pictac (t). **121 Dorling Kindersley:** Natural History Museum, London (tr). **Otorohanga Zoological Society (1980):** (bl). **124 Dr. Avishai Teicher:** (clb). **126 Alaska Fisheries Science Center, NOAA Fisheries Service:** (crb). **Pearson Asset Library:** Lord and Leverett / Pearson Education Ltd (cb). **Dreamstime.com:** John Anderson (cl); Ispace (fbl, bl, bc, br, fbr). **127 Dreamstime.com:** Ispace (bl, bc, br). **Photoshot:** NHPA / Paul Kay (cra). **130 Getty Images:** Jose Luis Pelaez Inc (c); Visuals Unlimited, Inc. / Joe McDonald (clb). **131 Corbis:** Minden Pictures / Suzi Eszterhas (b). **132 Corbis:** imagebroker / Konrad Wothe (cb). **Dreamstime.com:** Juri Bizgajmer (b/Reproduced four times). **Getty Images:** Joe McDonald (cl). **133 Corbis:** Wally McNamee (fclb); Robert Harding World Imagery / Thorsten Milse (clb). **Dreamstime.com:** Juri Bizgajmer (b/Reproduced three times). **Getty Images:** Daniel J. Cox (crb). **134 Science Photo Library:** Jim Zipp (bc). **134-135 Alamy Images:** Matthew Clarke. **136-137 Alamy Images:** Transtock Inc. (c). **137 Corbis:** Paul Souders (clb). **Dreamstime.com:** F9photos (tl). Getty Images: Ronald C. Modra (bl). **138 Alamy Images:** Bluegreen Pictures / David Shale (clb). **Corbis:** Wim van Egmond (crb). **Dreamstime.com:** Ferdericb (ca). **naturepl.com:** David Shale (cr). **139 Dorling Kindersley:** Dolphin Research Center, Grassy Key, Florida, www.dolphins.org (ca); Natural History Museum, London (cl, cb). **Getty Images:** AFP (cla). **140 Alamy Images:**

Duncan Usher (cl). Dreamstime.com: Isselee (br). **141 Dreamstime.com:** Georgii Dolgykh (clb); Jezper (tl); Goce Risteski (cl). **144-145 Dreamstime.com:** Haider Yousuf. **146 Corbis:** epa / ULI DECK (crb); Transtock (clb). Dreamstime.com: Raja Rc (c). **Getty Images:** Bill Pugliano (cla). **146-147 Corbis:** Chris Crisman. **147 Corbis:** Icon SMI / J. Neil Prather (c). **148-149 Alstom Transportation:** P. Sautelet (c). Corbis: Imaginechina (cr). **148 Alamy Images:** Sagaphoto.com / Gautier Stephane (c). Getty Images: SSPL (cl). **150 Corbis:** George Hall (t). **150-151 Getty Images:** Marvin E. Newman (c). **151 Alamy Images:** LM (crb). **NASA:** (b). **152 Alamy Images:** DIZ Muenchen GmbH, Sueddeutsche Zeitung Photo (c). **Dreamstime.com:** Brutusman (clb). **153 Dreamstime.com:** Rui Matos (cl). **154-155 Getty Images:** AFP / MARCEL MOCHET. **154 Getty Images:** Bryn Lennon (b). **157 Dreamstime.com:** Richard Koele (b). **Royal Caribbean Cruises Ltd.:** (tr). **158 123RF.com:** 3ddock (clb). **Dreamstime.com:** Chernetskiy (b/Reproduced two times). **158-159 A.P. Moller/ Maersk:** (c). **159 Dockwise:** (tr). **160 Alamy Images:** Dennis Hallinan (c). **161 Corbis:** Morton Beebe (c/Boeing). **NASA:** (br). **163 NASA:** (cb). **164 Science Photo Library:** Ria Novosti (clb). **168-169 Corbis:** Science Faction / Louie Psihoyos (finger). **169 Alamy Images:** David J. Green (crb). **170 Dreamstime.com:** Marekp (cb). **Sebastian Loth, CFEL Hamburg, Germany:** (bl). **175 Getty Images:** Barcroft Media / Imre Solt (br). **177 Corbis:** Ed Kashi (tr). **178-179 Getty Images:** Charles Bowman (c). **179 Getty Images:** Edward L. Zhao (tr). **184 Alamy Images:** Giffard Stock (clb)

All other images
© Dorling Kindersley

For further information see:
www.dkimages.com